Career Success Workbook

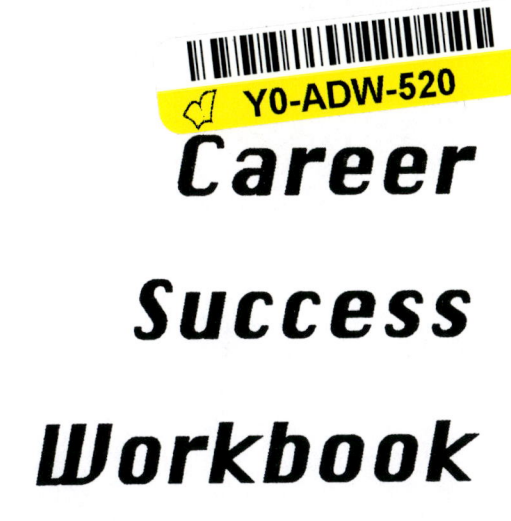

John Elson and Dick Wright

Copyright Statement

The CAREER SUCCESS WORKBOOK that you are reading is the result of Dick Wright's and John Elson's individual and collective efforts encompassing more than two decades.

This includes: research; personal experience in career assessment, development training, and counseling; teaching CAREER SUCCESS seminars; conducting job support groups for unemployed individuals; and lots of helpful feedback from our clients.

We have intentionally created a book which is to be "worked on" versus being read. Since this workbook will serve you best as a practical tool — one you can refer to and work on over time — we have designed it with ample space to complete the exercises and write notes.

PLEASE DO NOT TAKE ADVANTAGE OF OUR EFFORTS BY PHOTOCOPYING ANY PORTION OF THIS BOOK.

Should you be interested in purchasing additional copies of the book for yourself, your friends, or family, OR in being added to our mailing list, please complete the form at the back of the book.

We also encourage you to contact us with comments at:
ELSON/WRIGHT ASSOCIATES
ROLLING MEADOWS OFFICE
3306 S. ORIOLE LANE
ROLLING MEADOWS, IL 60008
708-398-0640

WE HOPE YOU ENJOY THE BOOK!!

©All material copyrighted and registered with the U.S. Government Copyright Office, 1992, by John B. Elson and M. Richard Wright. All rights reserved.

ISBN 0-9634053-0-6

Acknowledgements

No one can author a book in a vacuum. We are therefore grateful to the following individuals without whose support and assistance this Workbook would not have been possible:

- Participants in our Career Success courses whose candid comments and insightful recommendations helped shape each successive translation of the course as well as the sequence and presentation of the Workbook;

- Cindy Clontz, Director of the Wright College Economic Development Center, who gave us the opportunity to present the course on a regular basis and helped us to explain it to the public;

- Bob Picha, who introduced us to "DISC Theory" and its application to work style;

- Jane Ulrich, who tirelessly and meticulously created and implemented the formatting of this volume;

- Ginny Elson and Bob Elson for their efforts in developing our mailing list and providing a sounding board for our ideas;

- Our wives, Ellen Elson and Pat Wright, for their unfailing encouragement, timely suggestions and wisdom.

THIS WORKBOOK IS DEDICATED TO THE MEMORY OF ADAM ELSON AND HELEN WRIGHT.

Career Success Workbook

Table of Contents

Chapter	Title	Page
	Introduction: Your Journey Begins	6

The Overview Dimension

1	Master Career Planning: The Path to Career Success	11
2	Assessing Your Career	37

The Individual Dimension

3	Understanding Work Styles	47
4	Profiling Your Work Style	59
5	Profiling Your Current & Ideal Jobs: What Makes You Happy?	65
6	Assessing and Profiling Your Skills	73

The Personal Marketing Dimension

7	Proactivity	105
8	Developing Your Resume and Cover Letter	117
9	Fine Tuning Your Image and Behavior	145
10	Reading and Responding to Another's Work Style	157
11	Preparing for Your Interview	165
	Summary: Your Journey Continues	181
	Index	187

Introduction: Your Journey Begins

You are about to begin a workbook. It means just that — a book to be worked in, not read from cover to cover as you would a novel. It is a book for you to *interact with* from start to finish.

The Workbook is *self-paced*, which means you proceed at your own speed, level of tolerance and motivation. We want you to get involved immediately — to begin to use the many exercises which will assist you to achieve our collective objective: your initial Master Career Plan. This Plan will move you forward **now** toward your first job or your next position, whether within or outside of your current company.

Whether you are currently working or not, whether you are currently satisfied with your present job or not, whatever age you are — this workbook is for YOU! It is never too late (or too early, for that matter) to begin the exciting adventure of growing in self awareness and truly taking control of your life!

The workbook is *systematic* in that it moves in a logical progression from one stage in our process to the next. It provides you with all the tools you will need to assist you in developing your Master Career Plan not only now but throughout the remainder of your working days.

When all is said and done, there are only two kinds of people: those who take control of their lives and those who don't! This workbook is meant for the "control takers" — for you! Your task is to TAKE CONTROL of the decision-making process related to your career choices for the rest of your life.

Is this a one-time process that, once completed, will automatically carry you through the rest of your life? Absolutely not! Master Career Planning is a lifelong undertaking. This workbook will get you started — get you "on the road". But a key component of the process is for you to periodically (by that we mean at least once a year) review your status, determine where you want to go, and thereby refine your career progression. Think of this process as your annual Personal Performance Review in which you sit down with your notes from the last review and take stock of where you've gone over the past year, as well as identify goals and an action plan for where you want to go during the next year.

THUS WE HOPE YOU WILL REFER TO THESE PAGES NOT ONLY AT THIS POINT IN TIME BUT REGULARLY THEREAFTER AS YOU CONTINUE TO TAKE CONTROL OVER YOUR OWN CAREER PROGRESSION.

We'll be there to support you each step of the way as your journey progresses.

Start now by identifying what you expect to get from this workbook. Place your responses on the next page.

My Expectations

Take a moment now to respond to this question: Briefly, what do you expect to have accomplished after you have finished this Workbook?

1. _____

2. _____

3. _____

4. _____

What did you write down? Increased Self Confidence...Greater Control over your Life...A More Positive Self Image...? Keep your initial expectations in mind as you continue through this workbook. We will ask you to refer back to this list when you begin Chapter 9, "Fine Tuning Your Image and Behavior".

The Overview Dimension

It is more important to live the life one wishes to live and to go down with it if necessary, quite contentedly, than to live more profitably but less happily.

-Marjorie Kinnan Rawlings

Chapter 1 Master Career Planning: the Path to Career Success

What Is Master Career Planning?

It is the process of creating an overview for your career. This refers to a broad, conceptual approach for determining the best path for your career. This means that you will map out an approach for yourself which is based on a review of nine different components (See Components of the Master Career Planning Process on the next page).

These components comprise the nine fundamental areas of importance to clearly understand where you're headed. Master Career Planning is the first concept in your approach to Career Success.

MASTER CAREER PLANNING REALLY WORKS!

The overwhelming success of our CAREER SUCCESS seminars and our individual career assessment counseling has provided us tremendous insight into the nature of current career pursuits.

The concept of Master Career Planning is the result of years of research and application by ELSON/WRIGHT ASSOCIATES with hundreds of individuals that work in a variety of different careers.

Components of the Master Career Planning Process

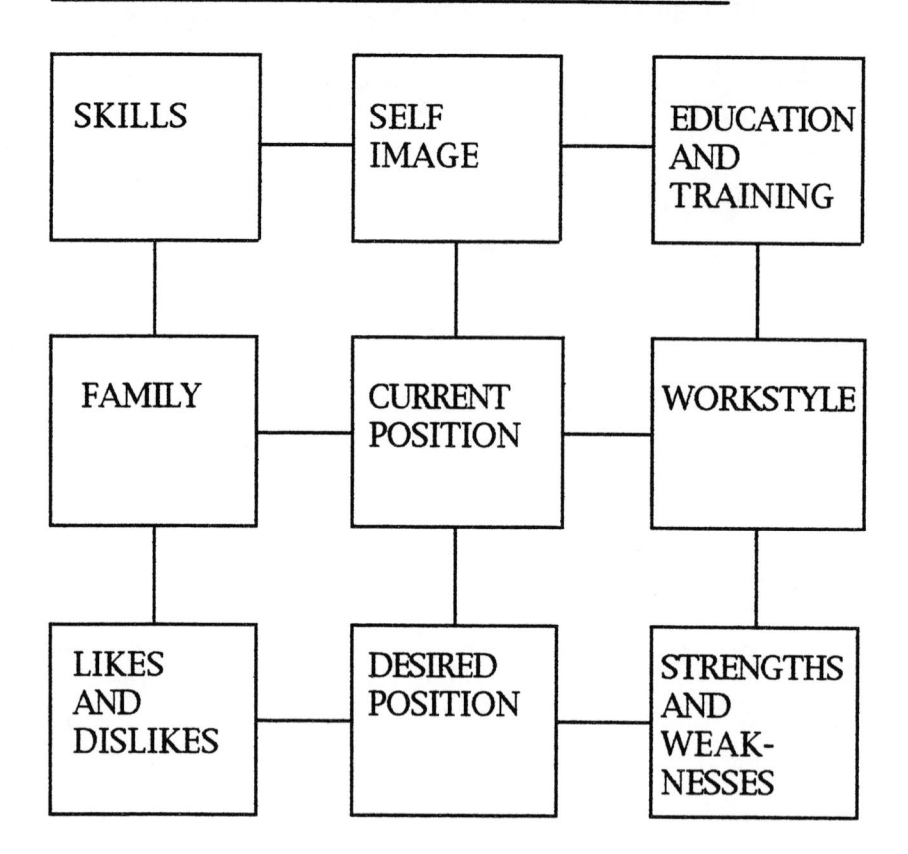

SKILLS	SELF IMAGE	EDUCATION AND TRAINING
FAMILY	CURRENT POSITION	WORKSTYLE
LIKES AND DISLIKES	DESIRED POSITION	STRENGTHS AND WEAK-NESSES

The Four Major Steps to Career Success

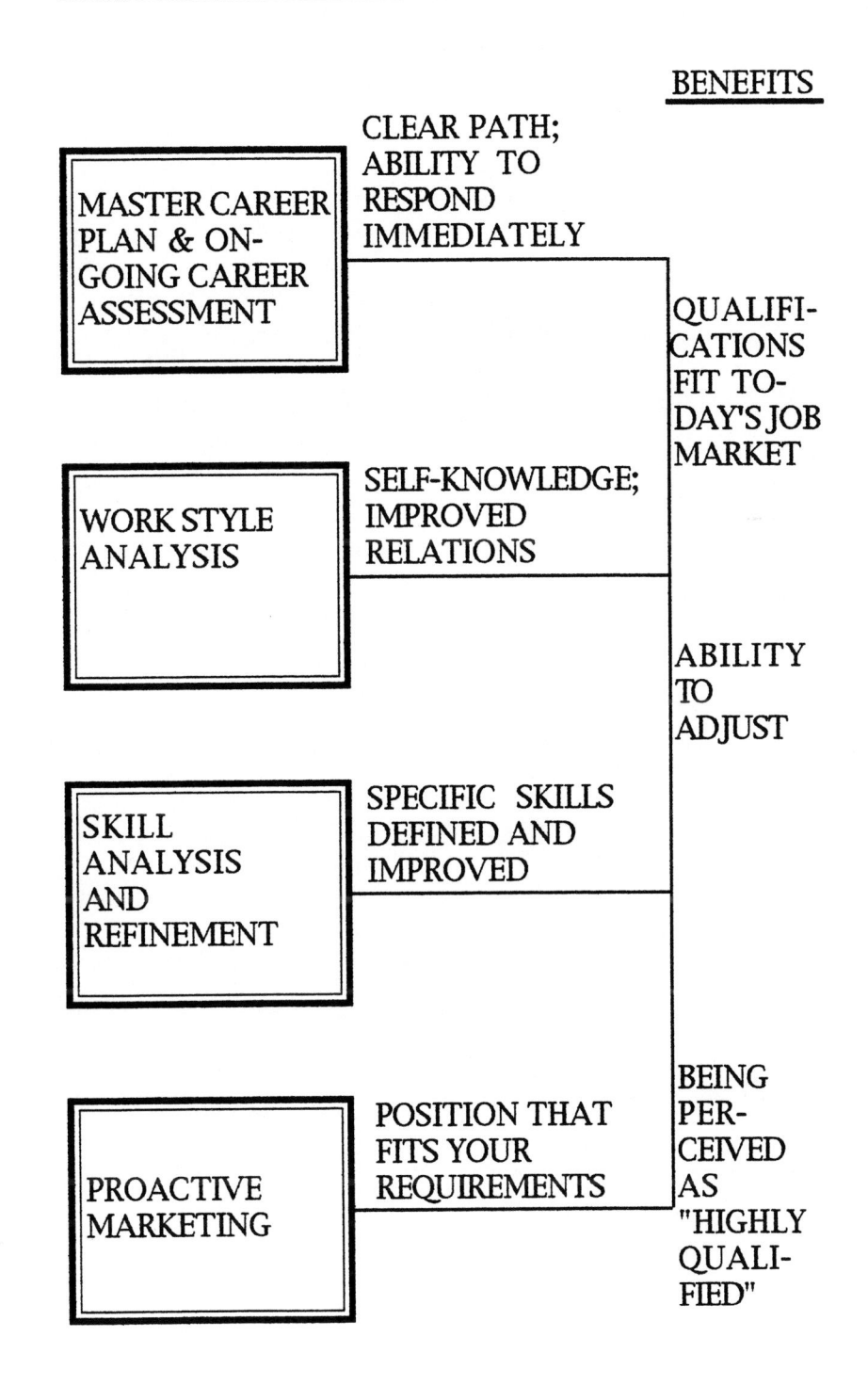

BENEFITS

MASTER CAREER PLAN & ON-GOING CAREER ASSESSMENT	CLEAR PATH; ABILITY TO RESPOND IMMEDIATELY	QUALIFI-CATIONS FIT TODAY'S JOB MARKET
WORK STYLE ANALYSIS	SELF-KNOWLEDGE; IMPROVED RELATIONS	ABILITY TO ADJUST
SKILL ANALYSIS AND REFINEMENT	SPECIFIC SKILLS DEFINED AND IMPROVED	
PROACTIVE MARKETING	POSITION THAT FITS YOUR REQUIREMENTS	BEING PERCEIVED AS "HIGHLY QUALIFIED"

As you see on Page 13 (Exhibit entitled THE FOUR MAJOR STEPS TO CAREER SUCCESS), the development of the MASTER CAREER PLAN is interrelated with ON-GOING CAREER ASSESSMENT, a concept which we will discuss in greater detail both later in this chapter and in Chapter 2.

Developing a MASTER CAREER PLAN will provide you with several long-term benefits:

- A Clear Path from which you can accurately gauge and review career opportunities;

- The ability to respond immediately when presented with a job offer, geographical transfer, promotion or new position;

- Qualifications which fit today's job market versus choosing a career for merely emotional reasons. Emotional reasons are those such as it "feels right" or "it's the right thing to do", or "my parents always told me I should be a lawyer and I'm finally going to do it," etc.;

- A greatly improved sense of satisfaction and self confidence.

WHAT ADDITIONAL BENEFITS COME TO MIND?

_____

_____

_____

_____

_____

These benefits will last a lifetime if you diligently apply what you learn from this workbook and if you refer to your exercises FREQUENTLY

AND REGULARLY OVER THE COURSE OF YOUR CAREER.

But remember, no workbook is a panacea! You must be willing to commit both time and effort to the process of expanding your "Career Consciousness". WITHOUT COMMITMENT AND EFFORT ON YOUR PART, YOUR RETURN WILL BE LESS THAN IT COULD BE.

Why Should You Plan?

Today's job market is perhaps the most volatile in the history of the United States. Recent statistics indicate that the average worker remains in a job/position for 3.4 years. This rapid turnover of positions means that it is very likely that you will hold between five and ten positions over the course of your career!

This is significantly different than fifty years ago in the United States when the economy was dictated heavily by the second World War and when the Computer Age was a fantasy.

The stability of the job market was predictable and a fact of life at that time. It was not unusual for a businessperson to remain with one company for an entire career.

This job stability provided workers with greater predictability in their careers. But, like most things in life, along with stability came several negatives: less APPARENT choice, fewer career paths to review and a more drone-like existence for many people.

In fact, many individuals that lived and worked during this period indicate that they didn't feel they had any REAL choice regarding their jobs.

"We just worked and that was that." Individuals back then didn't have the resources or the opportunities that we have today. Many never considered the prospect of moving to a new position.

Coupled with the fact that 20% more women are working than just twenty years ago, and almost two thirds of all the new entrants to the workforce between 1987 and 2000 will be women, our employment market has undergone phenomenal change over the last two decades. In fact, 60% of all women will be working by the year 2000, and organizations will be changing dramatically to accommodate rapidly changing demographics in other areas as well.

Just as the globalization of the world is beginning to heavily influence our own economy, business dynamics have been affected by world trends, changing consumer preferences, dramatic shifts in demography and the everpresent pressure of profit and loss.

Like it or not, we are part of a job market which is changing very rapidly. We call these shifts and changes "Market Dynamics." A recent article in Fortune magazine by Kenneth Labich discussed the market dynamics of today's environment and stated "You've got to take control of your career and manage it. You are your own business."

This necessitates an approach to your career which centers around PLANNING. Traditionally viewed as an ivory tower concept reserved for senior managers and boardrooms, planning is a critical component in any successful career. However, THE PLANNING THAT WE ENDORSE BEGINS LONG BEFORE:

- You first enter the job market;
- You anticipate leaving your current job;
- Your job is terminated.

The current job market necessitates on-going career assessment and planning, which underscores the need to remain alert and ready for the next opportunity.

As John Wooden, famous basketball coach for the UCLA Bruins (and one of the greatest coaches in college history) said: LUCK IS WHEN PREPARATION MEETS OPPORTUNITY.

This statement is critical. Be certain you understand that when it comes to career progression, YOU MUST TAKE RESPONSIBILITY FOR YOUR OWN DESTINY. That is, your career goal should fit in with a defined path that you create and that you change, as appropriate, during your journey.

You must follow a "journey mentality" in your career, versus a "destination mentality." This is carved out beautifully in Robert Hastings essay, "THE STATION." Please read Hastings' essay (Pages 18 and 19) right now.

Hastings' concept of enjoying the journey is the key to career success. Yet the career journey cannot be one of random sights. You must develop an initial plan, and then massage your plan, as needed, on an on-going basis. In this way, you will assure yourself that you are at least "headed for the right city".

This brings us right back to the idea of On-Going Career Assessment. On-Going Career Assessment is an advanced concept in Career Planning. Essentially, it means that you review the forces which impact your career on an on-going basis.

"The Station"

Tucked away in our subconscious is an idyllic vision. We see ourselves on a long trip that spans the continent. We are travelling by train. Out the windows we drink in the passing scene of cars on nearby highways, of children waving at a crossing, of cattle grazing on a distant hillside, of smoke pouring from a power plant, of row upon row of corn and wheat, of flatlands and valleys, of mountains and rolling hillsides, of city skylines and village halls.

But uppermost in our minds is the final destination. On a certain day at a certain hour we will pull into the station. Bands will be playing and flags waving. Once we get there so many wonderful dreams will come true and the pieces of our lives will fit together like a completed jigsaw puzzle. How restlessly we pace the aisles, damning the minutes for loitering—waiting, waiting, waiting for the station.

"When we reach the station, that will be it!" we cry. "When I'm 18." "When I buy a new 450 SL Mercedes-Benz!" "When I put the last kid through college." "When I have paid off the mortgage!" "When I get a promotion." "When I reach the age of retirement, I shall live happily ever after!"

Sooner or later we must realize there is no station, no one place to arrive at once and for all. The true joy of life is the trip. The station is only a dream. It constantly outdistances us.

"Relish the moment" is a good motto, especially when coupled with Psalm 118:24: "This is the day which the Lord hath made; we will rejoice and be glad in it." It isn't the burdens of today that drive men mad. It is the regrets over yesterday and the fear of tomorrow. Regret and fear are twin thieves who rob us of today.

So, stop pacing the aisles and counting the miles. Instead, climb more mountains, eat more ice cream, go barefoot more often, swim more rivers, watch more sunsets, laugh more, cry less. Life must be lived as we go along. The station will come soon enough.

— by Robert J. Hastings

This is necessary for at least two reasons:

- It will provide you with a much wider perspective on your career in that you will always know where you are in relation to the current marketplace and;

- It will allow you to move very rapidly to "catch an opportunity" that presents itself.

Therefore, THE MAIN THEME OF OUR WORKBOOK IS: THERE IS NO SUBSTITUTE FOR SELF-KNOWLEDGE.

Let's discuss and review the basics of the CAREER ASSESSMENT METHODOLOGY AS WE SEE IT (SEE Page 21, THE 6-POINT LIST CALLED THE SIX ASPECTS OF CAREER ASSESSMENT).

The heart of On-Going Career Assessment is PROACTIVITY, a topic which we discuss in greater detail in Chapter 7. For the moment, however, the key is to realize that proactivity is far different than reactivity. Proactivity means that you take control of your own career instead of assuming that someone else is looking out for your best interests. Unfortunately, the chances are that they are not.

Your own personal proactivity has already been demonstrated by your purchase of this workbook. Rather than waiting for the job market to come to you, you've come to the job market.

The Six Aspects of Career Assessment

- INTROSPECTION
- DOCUMENTATION
- REFLECTION
- PLANNING
- PROACTIVITY
- PROGRESS REVIEW

This personal choice is a main ingredient to career success and the basis for our entire CAREER SUCCESS course.

It is critical that you FULLY UNDERSTAND these major concepts before we move into a discussion of just how to develop your first version of a MASTER CAREER PLAN.

Introspection

Introspection, a term used extensively in self-development circles, identifies the process that each individual undergoes to learn more about himself/herself BY LOOKING WITHIN. This self-reflection, or mirroring, can range anywhere from minimal to extremely detailed and deep, often depending on the individual's own personality and current psychological environment. Introspection involves the integration of external stimuli, information and knowledge and their application to help define "who you are".

It is commonly felt that different individuals are "more" or "less" introspective in terms of their willingness and interest in TURNING WITHIN to understand themselves.

As it relates to this workbook, it is extremely important that you make every attempt to open yourself up to self-review and to change. IF YOU RESIST THE IDEAS AND CONCEPTS, YOU WILL REDUCE THEIR BENEFIT.

Documentation

This refers to the term as you already know it, that is, to record, in some fashion, as a permanent record, events, feelings, ideas and emotions as they relate to your career. You can document in two ways:

- Formally writing the ideas in a journal, or;

- Maintaining a library of micro cassettes or cassettes which you record with a dictaphone or a tape recorder.

Documentation allows you to retain a record of your thoughts, ideas, and, particularly your feelings regarding a given work situation, environment or work style.

The work styles of your co-workers, including your boss and subordinates, are extremely important. They are discussed throughout this workbook and are detailed in Chapter 3.

Reflection

Reflection refers to the process of considering what you have already thought about, but in a more open and relaxed manner.

When you reflect on something, you consider the thought across a broad range of possibilities. One way to achieve reflective thinking is to consider the thought simply as the thought itself, that is, without any constraints of time, sensibility, or judgment.

Right now, just think about a pool of water. What image does it convey to you? It should be just the image of the water, without any additions, environmental considerations, or constraints.

This process is effective in maintaining clarity and keeping you on course regarding your career thoughts. Once you have used INTROSPECTION and DOCUMENTATION, REFLECTION allows you to reconsider the bare idea just to see it as an idea. Then you can move forward by adding considerations to it. In this way, you are not masking or altering the basic idea until it has been considered on its own merits. This is difficult to do, but well worth the effort, as a means of reducing personal bias.

For example, let's say that you've been "introspecting" and you've documented all the characteristics that you feel are necessary to be a SUCCESSFUL STOCKBROKER.

When you REFLECT on the idea, what images come into your mind? Write those images below:

_____

_____

_____

_____

_____

Once you develop a clear image, you can attach constraints in any manner that you choose, such as:

- The current employment scene;
- The projected fit as it relates to your personality, or;
- The organization's overall style and image.

If the image alone provides a positive and rewarding view, then, and only then can you realistically alter it by considering the path of friends that you know who are stockbrokers, or the advice of other people. Now, let's take a specific career that YOU have been considering for yourself.

CAREER _____

Reflect on this career. Start by writing unencumbered ideas that come to mind when you consider the career.

_____

_____

_____

_____

Now, add concepts and ideas that gradually alter your view, such as "your concept of the job market for this career", "your specific view of others that you know who hold this career" or "your view of what it would require to get a job of this type".

Planning

Planning, as we have already seen, is at the heart of our entire methodology. To plan, and to keep planning, is the key to career success. In this way, you will always be prepared to shift as your situation requires.

Proactivity

Our definition of proactivity is "The initiation of thoughts, plans and activities by an individual based on his/her personal motivation."

Proactivity refers to the process of initiating action. As we have discussed previously, proactivity is critical to career progression and is essentially the opposite of reactivity. It refers to taking control of your destiny. We'll discuss it in detail in Chapter 7.

Progress Review

The term Progress Review can mean many things. In the context of the our methodology, it refers to the regular review of the progress that you are making in understanding your self, your career aspirations and your course of direction. It can be augmented by "Reality Checks" whereby you sit down with a friend, family member or counselor and present your idea of what you have chosen.

Your "listener" then serves as a "devil's advocate", asking questions and making comments to help determine whether what you have chosen is sensible within the context of the current job market, your training, your skills, etc.

Identify a person right now that will serve as your "listener" and establish when you will meet with that person.

Name of Listener

_____

Date By Which I Will Meet

_____

Developing Your Master Career Plan

Let's start to work!

A Master Career Plan is a working document. It will serve as the basis for your career decisions by providing a reference that you can read, edit and refer to over the course of your career. Once you've prepared your initial MASTER CAREER PLAN, you'll probably want to modify it after completing the remainder of this workbook. DON'T BE DISCOURAGED! Remember you are not developing a final, complete document, but rather the first draft of an on-going "working document".

Your initial plan is developed early in the workbook so that you will understand that it is comprised of all facets of our approach. We suggest that you revise your first draft immediately after completing the workbook. In that way, your new ideas and thoughts will still be fresh in your mind.

Please read the next page; it describes how to prepare your MASTER CAREER PLAN. Then, follow the guidelines on the page after it.

Example Components of a Master Career Plan

MISSION STATEMENT (STEPS 1-3)

- Prepare a statement which accurately describes the nature of your career mission, including why, when and how it will be achieved.

OBJECTIVE (STEP 4)

- Establish an objective which is consistent with your current position, interests and capabilities. If a disability or other issue is involved, consider the physical limitations of the position and its impact on your "personal gauge system."

- Prepare a summary of the positions that you will aspire to and the time frame connected to each one.

SELF-CHECK (STEP 5)

- Utilize a friend, family member or counselor to assist you with the "reality check" to see if what you have established makes sense for you.

IMPLEMENTATION (STEP 6)

- Document the activities which you will be required to perform in order to carry out your plan. Be specific and include timeframes along with expected completion dates.

- Initiate the process by carving out small components and starting to work on one activity.

Step 1: Prepare Your Mission Statement

Your mission statement should accurately describe the nature of your career mission, including why, when and how it will be achieved.

A complete example is: " My goal over the next five years is to become the Manager of Accounting in a manufacturing company with sales of at least $50 million per year. My rationale for this decision is based on my current position as Senior Accountant with the Q Company, a $20 million producer of flight widgets for the aerospace industry and my interest and enjoyment in pursuing an accounting career. I believe that a larger company will provide me with:

- Better training and supervisory opportunities;

- A more expansive career path;

- Better near-term compensation, and;

- The ability to deal with more sophisticated information and related systems."

NOW, START YOUR FIRST BASIC MISSION STATEMENT. Try to simply establish the specific nature of your quest without qualifying time constraints or related support.

MY MISSION IS:

_____

_____

_____

_____

_____

_____

_____

_____

_____

_____

_____

_____

Step 2: Describe and Support Your Proposed Time Frame

"I will achieve the position of Manager of Accounting within three years. This includes two more years as Senior Accountant and a third year as a buffer if I am not promoted in my first attempt."

NEXT, DESCRIBE YOUR PROPOSED TIME FRAME:

_____

_____

_____

_____

_____

Step 3: Establish the "How"

For example: "I will study Accounting at night by taking a course each quarter at the local college. I intend to have all courses completed in two years to prepare me to take the C.P.A. exam in the Fall of 1995. I will work at least fifty to sixty hours a week at my job and I intend to volunteer for all special assignments presented by the Chief Financial Officer."

NOW, ESTABLISH YOUR "HOW":

_____

_____

_____

_____

_____

_____

_____

_____

Step 4: *Establish a Near-Term Objective*

THE NEXT STEP TO AN EFFECTIVE MASTER CAREER PLAN IS TO ESTABLISH A NEAR-TERM OBJECTIVE. This objective must be reasonable, achievable and realizable within a time frame of one to two years. For example: "I will attempt to be promoted to Experienced Senior Accountant by the end of this year. This is consistent with my current position, interests and capabilities. In order to achieve this, I need to be responsible for three major projects within the next nine months. I will make arrangements with my superior to meet and discuss how this may be achieved."

If you are currently working, make sure that this objective fits in with your current boss' perception and that it fits well with your current set of performance appraisals. Obviously, if this isn't realistic, establish an objective which is more realistic.

In some cases, if your current position isn't going quite the way you'd like, it may be sensible to PLAN TO DISCUSS IT WITH YOUR SUPERIOR, AN ADVISOR OR ANOTHER COMPANY PROFESSIONAL, such as a HUMAN RESOURCES PROFESSIONAL. If you have already determined that you have exhausted all avenues, perhaps your objective should be to leave your company.

This can be a reasonable objective, as long as you have given appropriate consideration to both WHY you are leaving and WHAT will make you happy.

If you are not currently employed, make sure that this objective fits in with a realistic assessment of your self. You may want to discuss this idea with a friend, family member or advisor.

What is important here is that you establish a commitment to a verifiable time frame, and that you INITIATE ACTION TOWARDS THE ACHIEVEMENT OF THE OBJECTIVE.

PREPARE YOUR NEAR-TERM OBJECTIVES:

1. _____
_____
_____

2. _____
_____
_____

3. _____
_____
_____

4. _____
_____
_____

For each subsequent position within the context of your MASTER CAREER PLAN, you must establish time frames and paths of action. In this way you will be helping to move yourself along.

We have established five years as a reasonable length of time for your entire plan. This can, however, be modified to suit any length of time. It is suggested, however, that unless you are able to attach specific activities to your objectives, that you do not establish a Master Career Plan with a long-term mission such as "I want to be president of a company someday", especially if the "someday" is twenty years in the future. Not only is the time frame too long, but the objective may be totally unrealistic.

Step 5: Self-Check

Once you have completed the first steps in establishing the MASTER CAREER PLAN, you must "subject" the plan to self and outside examination. This means that you should first conduct an independent review of what you have written in order to determine:

- If it makes sense;
- Whether the choices are realistic, in keeping with your family issues, commitments, schedule and lifestyle;
- If your choices are consistent with today's job market and the future market as you perceive it.

Then, ask a friend, family member or counselor to review the plan and to serve as your confidant in a private "give and take" session.

The purpose of this session is to determine whether the individual feels that this path is appropriate for you based on his/her review and your answers to his/her questions.

Now, commit yourself to the completion of your self-check:

I will complete my own self-check on _____
                                           Date

I will meet with my external advisor on _____
                                              Date

Step 6: Implementation

The final step in developing your Master Career Plan is implementation. This is best accomplished by carving out small activities and attaching timeframes for completion.

For example, if your plan requires that you develop <u>specific</u> performance objectives for your position, in order to prepare to meet with your boss, plan to do this at a <u>specific</u> time for a <u>specific</u> period of time. For example, Wednesday from 8 to 10 a.m. In this way, you will start to approach the task in small pieces and it won't appear to be quite so large.

Once you understand Master Career Planning, you're ready to move forward. Chapter 2 discusses the importance of on-going career assessment.

The greatest thing you can find out is just how good you can be.

-Bill Russell

Chapter 2 Assessing Your Career

On-going career assessment, a concept which we introduced in the last chapter, accurately characterizes what YOU NEED TO DO IN TODAY'S EMPLOYMENT MARKETPLACE. IT IS NO LONGER SENSIBLE, AT ANY LEVEL, IN ANY SITUATION, TO SIT BACK AND WAIT BEFORE SERIOUSLY ADDRESSING THE DIRECTION OF YOUR CAREER. On-going career assessment and proactivity are two concepts that go hand-in-hand. They are the opposite of trauma-based career assessment and reactivity.

Please refer to the chart on the next page (Page 38).

Career Assessment

ON-GOING

The process of conducting a review of your career position on an on-going basis, taking proactive initiative, and creating a path of action.

ADVANTAGES

- Readily accessible information about who you are and where your skills may best be utilized

- A more relaxed attitude toward the future: the contentment that comes from self-knowledge

- The ability to set in motion and modify a MASTER CAREER PLAN

- Improved responsiveness to opportunities

TRAUMA-BASED

The process of waiting until something happens to you, such as being fired or laid-off from your job before considering the potential paths for your skill-set and career.

DISADVANTAGES

- The feeling of panic that sets in with being unprepared, especially in a potential crisis

- The possibility that you'll be caught without a plan as a result of your company's being sold or merged, or your being offered a transfer

- The likelihood that you will relegate your job search to positions that are currently available versus seeking out the best position

Now, let's look at how you start to effectively assess your career. First, please turn to Page 40. You'll notice on this chart two unusual terms: TANGIBLE TANGIBLES and INTANGIBLE TANGIBLES. Tangible Tangibles are those things which are usually thought of as very specific in terms of your current/future job. They include things like your benefit package, your title and the number of people in your company. They are the more QUANTITATIVE aspects of the job, such as:

TANGIBLE TANGIBLES

- Salary

- Bonus

- Title

- Executive Parking Space

- Office

- Personal Secretary

Intangible Tangibles are those things that are less specific such as your relationship with your boss, the similarity (or difference) in work styles between you and your boss or your perception of how your company treats its employees.

How to Evaluate Your Position As Well As Other Opportunities

TANGIBLE TANGIBLES

Medium Ego/High Reward:

- Total compensation

- Benefits:

    Profit sharing
    Stock plans
    Vacation
    Insurance
    Automobile
    Etc.

High Ego/Low Reward

- Title

- Number of direct reports

- Size of department

- Level within the department

- Budget size

- Etc.

INTANGIBLE TANGIBLES

- Your relationship with your supervisor
- Similarity or difference between your superior's management style and your own
- Similarity or difference between the company's strategic direction and your view of the best strategic direction
- Your perception of how the company treats its employees
- Your agreement/disagreement with the current level of communication presented by management to its employees
- Your perception of the company's public image
- Your perceived visibility within the company
- Your status with respect to others

Intangible Tangibles are more QUALITATIVE aspects of the job, such as:

INTANGIBLE TANGIBLES

- Your relationship with your boss

- Your level of agreement/disagreement with your company's strategic direction

- The management style of your boss in comparison to your own

- The organization's "culture"

- Your "comfort level" as to how the organization treats its employees

- The attitude of the organization toward change

In other words, intangible tangibles are more QUALITATIVE. The key to understanding the issues related to the current and future assessment of YOUR career is more easily understood by completing the exercises on Pages 43 and 44. In these exercises, you are asked to fill in the spaces by listing your tangible tangibles and intangible tangibles as you view them in your current position or, if you aren't currently working, in your most recent position (this may include part-time positions). You will notice that the chart on Page 43 is to be used for your Current Position (or most recent) and the second page is to be used for your perception of your Future Position.

This means that you can utilize this chart WHEN YOU ARE CONSIDERING A SPECIFIC POSITION THAT IS OFFERED TO YOU.

There are many advantages in listing the components. First, it allows you to focus on each concept individually and collectively. Second, because it is written on paper, you can retain it for your future records and reflect on your decision relative to its success. Third, it provides a great degree of flexibility in that you can compare positions with different dimensions by comparing the lists of tangible tangibles and intangible tangibles.

NOW, COMPLETE THE CHART ON PAGE 43. If you are also considering a new position, complete the chart on Page 44. Utilize the following directions:

1) LIST FIVE TANGIBLE TANGIBLES AND FIVE INTANGIBLE TANGIBLES. Be certain that these are the most important ones that you can think of in your current (most recent) position.

2) If you wish, expand your review by writing a detailed description of each characteristic that you list.

3) Once you have completed this exercise, you can use this format for any position that you consider or that you secure. It is a straightforward means for establishing and DOCUMENTING the issues of greatest importance to you.

Your Current Position

YOUR TANGIBLE TANGIBLES	YOUR INTANGIBLE TANGIBLES
1. _____	_____
_____	_____
2. _____	_____
_____	_____
3. _____	_____
_____	_____
4. _____	_____
_____	_____
5. _____	_____
_____	_____

Your Future Position

YOUR TANGIBLE TANGIBLES

YOUR INTANGIBLE TANGIBLES

1. _____

_____

2. _____

_____

3. _____

_____

4. _____

_____

5. _____

_____

The Individual Dimension

Chapter 3
Understanding Work Styles

Your journey begins with *self awareness*. It is very important to understand some key areas of your own personality — particularly, your work style, your skills, and your self image. In this chapter we will deal with work style, reserving skills and self image for later chapters.

Why is work style important? It is crucial to understand how you approach work, that is, how you "behave" in the work setting, what your work values are, how you approach both the "task" and the "people" aspects of work because understanding your work style will be helpful in choosing your future career path!

Everyone, including your boss, peers, and staff has a "work style". Understanding work style gives insight not only into your own style and behavior but also into others' styles and behaviors.

Let's get started. We'll begin with an exercise which will get you focused on behaviors — other people's behaviors.

On the following page you will see a list of 24 words. As you look at these words, choose EIGHT which describe people you tend to get along with or work well with (or both). Place check marks after those words in the "Most" column.

Now think about people you have difficulty in getting along with or do not work well with (or both). As you continue to look at this list of 24 words, choose EIGHT which describe the behaviors of those people and place the check marks in the column labelled "Least."

Other People's Behavior: A Checklist

The following words describe some of the behavioral tendencies of people.

Please read through the entire list. Then go back and check under the "Most" column EIGHT (8) words that describe people you tend to work with Most Effectively. Repeat the process, this time checking under the "Least" column EIGHT (8) words which describe people you tend to work with Least Effectively. Then briefly indicate Why you checked each item.

	Most	Least	Why Checked
1. Driving	___	___	_____
2. Pioneering	___	___	_____
3. Aggressive	___	___	_____
4. Demanding	___	___	_____
5. Domineering	___	___	_____
6. Competitive	___	___	_____
7. Charismatic	___	___	_____
8. Inspiring	___	___	_____
9. Self promoting	___	___	_____
10. Glib	___	___	_____
11. Impulsive	___	___	_____
12. Persuasive	___	___	_____
13. Accommodating	___	___	_____
14. Possessive	___	___	_____
15. Kind	___	___	_____
16. Self controlled	___	___	_____
17. Predictable	___	___	_____
18. Patient	___	___	_____
19. Conscientious	___	___	_____
20. Thorough	___	___	_____
21. Conventional	___	___	_____
22. Precise	___	___	_____
23. Diplomatic	___	___	_____
24. Perfectionistic	___	___	_____

You will notice that the 24 words are clustered into FOUR GROUPINGS, each grouping having 6 words. This fourfold grouping will serve to introduce the four different work styles.

Notice the configuration of the check marks you have placed. Do they tend to CLUSTER around one or two of the four groupings or are they more evenly distributed? We refer to this exercise later in this chapter, after you have gone through the work style exercise ON YOURSELF.

Overview of the Four Work Styles

There are four classic work styles which can be termed as follows: the "Directors"; the "Influencers"; the "Steady"; and the "Compliant".

The following chart provides an overview of the most obvious behaviors of each of the four work styles together with their basic intentions (that is, their primary work focus). Bear in mind as you consider the four work styles that every one of us (including yourself!) has at least a little of each of the four styles within us. Now take a look at the chart on the next page in order to get an "initial flavor" of each of the four work styles.

The Four Work Styles: An Overview

Style	Behavior	Intention
DIRECTORS (D)	• Aggressive • Forceful • Impatient • Direct	• To control the outcome • To control others
INFLUENCERS (I)	• Expressive • Talkative • Persuasive • Outgoing	• To attract attention • To persuade others
STEADY (S)	• Patient • Methodical • Low Key • Nondemonstrative	• To find security • To "fit in" with others
COMPLIANT (C)	• Detailed • Analytical • Critical • Precise	• To achieve perfection • To be left alone

"Directors"

People using this style act very sure of themselves. If you say, "You did a good job" they'll most likely say in return, "I know it." They tend to be very time conscious — lot's of things to accomplish in so little time! They're frustrated by a slow pace — people moving too slowly, talking too slowly, thinking too slowly. As a result, they tend to "finish" other people's sentences for them.

They focus on the task to be done, the "bottom line". Direct and to the point themselves, they want you to get right to the point — no beating around the bush! Concerned with the broad picture, they prefer not to get involved with "details". Their issue is "control" — not so much control of themselves but of everything and everyone else! They are very sensitive about how they are treated. They are uncomfortable with displays of emotion. They think in terms of strength and weakness; you are either strong or you are weak.

Their STRENGTHS include:

- Getting results
- Making decisions quickly
- Seeing the whole picture
- Making ideas happen
- Solving problems
- Self-assurance

Their WEAKNESSES can include:

- Impatience
- Ignoring details
- Being overly aggressive
- Acting too quickly
- Arrogance
- Snap judgments

"Influencers"

People using this style are outgoing and enjoy the company of others. They relish the opportunity to meet strangers. Quite optimistic — "the sun will come out tomorrow" — they display a lot of enthusiasm for what they're involved with. Oftentimes disorganized, they are not concerned with neatness and, like the Directors, are not interested in details.

They have an innate sense for the "climate" between people. They can tell very quickly whether there is tension within the group or whether the group gets along with each other. They feel confident they can talk anyone into anything. As a matter of fact, talking is their chief "tool". They love to have fun and are impressed by status and "image" — titles, offices, cars, anything which makes them look "good". They want people to like them.

Their STRENGTHS include:

- Ability to persuade others
- Ability to inspire others
- Social poise
- Verbal skill
- Ability to "read" others
- Self-confidence

Their WEAKNESSES can include:

- Overconfidence in their ability
- Poor listening skills
- Talking too much
- Too trusting of others
- Overly impulsive
- Wanting *everyone* to like them

"Steady"

People using this style undertake a project or task in a step-by-step fashion. They prefer to work on one task at a time until it is done; only then do they turn to the next task. They are very good at figuring out "how" to accomplish something, but they need time to think it all through.

They tend to resist change because change threatens their "security" which is a very important issue for them. Not knowing what the future will bring, particularly if they leave or lose their current job, is very upsetting to them. They are sincere and expect sincerity from others and are very loyal to their close friends and to people they trust.

They tend to establish relationships not only with people but also with objects and are very "possessive" about what is theirs — "this is my desk, my pencil, my report". They are truly "teamwork" minded — they pitch in when something needs to be done and provide support to (and look for support from) others. They tend to stay with things a long time — a job, a relationship, a task.

Their STRENGTHS include:

- Consistency in their behavior
- Consideration of others
- Self control
- Persistence
- Pitching in to help others
- Following through on projects

Their WEAKNESSES can include:

- Being resistant to change
- Being too lenient with others
- Complacency
- Taking on too much work
- Avoiding risks
- Following the crowd

"Compliant"

People using this style tend to be perfectionists — any flaw can tempt them to throw out the whole thing! They are very organized — "a place for everything and everything in its place". They revel in details and take lots of time to make decisions, preferring to wait until "all" the facts are in.

They are literal and precise and demand straightforward answers to their questions. They think of themselves as "realists", seeing exactly what is there — no more, no less. Like the "Steady", they resist change — their first question when asked to change is always "Why?" Taking great pride in their work ("my work represents me"), they are concerned about criticism from others, probably because they are already their own toughest critics. They focus on the task to be done and tend to be very serious about life and what is expected of them.

Their STRENGTHS include:

- Thoroughness
- Conscientiousness
- Being well-disciplined
- Precision
- Being diplomatic with others
- Accuracy

Their WEAKNESSES can include:

- Getting bogged down in details
- Not letting go until it's "perfect"
- Being too dependent on rules
- Tendency to worry
- Seeing things in black and white
- Being rigid and unyielding

The People in My Life

TURN YOUR ATTENTION AT THIS POINT TO SOME OF THE OTHER PEOPLE IN YOUR LIFE. Indicate below the predominant style of each of the significant people you deal with.

Person	Predominant Style
My current boss	_____
My last boss	_____
My best friend	_____
My spouse	_____
My coworkers (peers)	
_____	_____
_____	_____
_____	_____
My staff	
_____	_____
_____	_____
_____	_____
Others	
_____	_____
_____	_____
_____	_____

Style Interaction

As you have documented, everyone, (including yourself) your boss, your coworkers, your staff, has a style! How well do each of these workstyles INTERACT WITH each other? The following chart provides a guide to this important question. Two dimensions are reflected on the chart: how well the styles tend to get along with (or like) each other (the "L") and how well they tend to work together (the "W").

Notice that the styles which tend to both get along well with each other and work well together tend to be the "Steady" and the "Compliant". The styles with whom people tend to have more difficulty in getting along are the "Directors" and, ironically, the "Influencers."

The implications of this chart are quite important in terms of how you get along with others. "Directors" and the "Steady" sometimes have problems with each other revolving around the issues of change, speed of response, details, and the answer to the "Steady" style question "How?" (which the "Directors" are usually not interested in). "Influencers" and the "Compliant" sometimes have problems with each other revolving around the issues of quality, details, people versus task orientation, optimism versus realism, being organized and precise, and "wasting time".

Work Style Interaction

Style Combinations	Excellent	Good	Fair	Poor
D—D		L	W	
D—I		L	W	
D—S	W		L	
D—C			W	L
I—I	L			W
I—S	W		L	
I—C	W			L
S—S	L	W		
S—C	L	W		
C—C	L	W		

KEY: L = How well they GET ALONG with each other
W = How well they WORK with each other

57

At this point take another look at the checklist, "Other People's Behavior" which you completed on Page 48. You will now realize that the first set of words (#1-6) characterize the "Directors", the second set (#7-12) the "Influencers", the third set (#13-18) the "Steady", and the fourth set (#19-24) the "Compliant". Do the words you checked and why you checked them "say" anything to you about your compatibility with others' styles? Are there "clusters" of check marks under one or more sets of words? If there are clusters in the "Most" column this gives you insight into styles YOU TEND TO WORK WELL WITH. If there are clusters in the "Least" column this gives you some insight into styles YOU WORK LEAST WELL WITH. This is important information for you to keep in mind in terms of future relationships with others in the work setting, including your current boss as well as future bosses.

Reflecting on that exercise, complete the following:

Styles I tend to get along best with are

_____

_____

Styles I tend to get along least with are

_____

_____

Chapter 4
Profiling Your Work Style

Now that you have a "flavor" of each of the styles, which style do you believe MOST ACCURATELY describes you?

_____

_____

Which style LEAST ACCURATELY describes you?

_____

_____

On the next page you will have a chance to think about your own work behaviors in somewhat greater detail. AS YOU PREPARE TO COMPLETE THIS EXERCISE KEEP IN MIND THAT THERE ARE NO RIGHT OR WRONG ANSWERS. The only answer that "counts" is the answer you truly believe describes you as you are at this point in time, not as you want to be.

In addition, you must FOCUS on one situation in your life, namely yourself in the WORK SETTING, and STAY FOCUSED on that situation until you finish the profile. If you are not currently employed, focus on your most recent job, either full time or part time. The important point here is to FOCUS ON YOURSELF IN ONE SITUATION and to MAINTAIN that focus throughout!!

My Work Behaviors

Step 1: CIRCLE each of the following words or phrases which you think describe your behavior either on your current job or on your most recently held job.

Step 2: then, COUNT the number of circles in each group and record that number on the line under eachGroup.

AT WORK, I...

- Crave variety
- Like to be in charge
- Get bored with repetition
- Am often impatient
- Like to take risks
- Have a bias for action
- Am decisive
- Like challenge
- Am sensitive about how treated
- Like to outdo others

TOTAL GROUP 1 ____

- Desire social recognition
- Am optimistic
- Meet strangers easily
- Can inspire others
- Am the center of attention
- Seek fun/enjoyment
- Am status conscious
- Like to talk
- Am easy to be with
- Am persuasive

TOTAL GROUP 2 ____

- Am cautious
- Am sensitive about my work
- Strive for perfection
- Seek "right" answers
- Am self-controlled
- Know how things "fit"
- Hold high standards
- Follow rules & regulations
- Consider all alternatives
- Don't talk unless I'm sure

TOTAL GROUP 4 ____

- Am predictable
- Do one thing at a time
- Am willing to pitch in
- Want a secure environment
- Desire to "fit in"
- Am responsive to others
- Am persistent
- Like to work in one place
- Avoid conflict
- Am hesitant to speak up

TOTAL GROUP 3 ____

Remember that there are no "good" or "bad" results to this exercise. There are no "good" or "bad" styles. You are what you are and that's "ok". Just as the comic strip character, Popeye, was fond of saying, "I am what I am what I am what I am," so WE ARE WHAT WE ARE, with all our strengths and weaknesses, and should be proud of being "who we are."

You have totaled each of the four groups on the previous page. The group with the highest total is your preferred work style, the style you are MOST COMFORTABLE with. The group with the lowest total is your least preferred work style, the style you are LEAST COMFORTABLE with. You probably realize by now that Group 1 describes characteristics of the "Director" Style, Group 2 the characteristics of the "Influencer" style, Group 3 the "Steady" style and Group 4 the "Compliant" style. Rank your work styles below in descending order from your highest group total to your lowest group total:

MY WORK STYLES from high to low are:

HIGHEST TOTAL   ___ =   WORK STYLE
                                    _____

NEXT HIGHEST TOTAL   ___ =   WORK STYLE
                                    _____

THIRD HIGHEST TOTAL ___ =   WORK STYLE
                                    _____

LOWEST TOTAL   ___ =   WORK STYLE
                                    _____

The "highs" (namely, the numbers on those of your groups which total six or higher) capture the style or styles you tend to use the most. On the other hand the "lows" (namely, the numbers on those of your groups that total five or less) capture the style or styles you tend to use the least.

In this workbook we will deal at length with the behaviors of the "highs". However, the key point to keep in mind about the "lows" is that the style or styles that are low describe the styles with their characteristic behaviors which you tend to use the least. The reason you probably tend to avoid these styles is that for whatever reason you probably are not comfortable with them!! This is important for you to know because sometimes in order to be effective with another person you may need to behave in a way you may not be comfortable with. BEING ABLE TO ADAPT YOUR BEHAVIORS IN ORDER TO PRESENT THE IMAGE YOU WISH TO PRESENT is a very important skill which, as we discuss in Chapter 10, will make you MORE EFFECTIVE in dealing with employment interviewers as well as others in your life.

Today's preparation determines tomorrow's achievement.

-Anonymous

Chapter 5
Profiling Your Current & Ideal Jobs

It is now time to look at another important aspect of your life — YOUR JOB. Just as you were able to profile your own work style you will now profile your current or most recent job. Using the exercise found on the next page, think about the characteristics of your current job or most recent job and follow the instructions.

My Current Job

Listed below are a number of characteristics applicable to a variety of jobs. Please respond to each and every item listed by ranking its relative importance as you see it to the successful performance of the job you currently hold (or have recently held). Use the following scale to rank each and every item:

1 Not important
2 Low importance
3 High importance
4 Very high importance

Rank

___ Diplomacy & tact
___ Gather detailed information
___ Follow quality standards
___ Adhere to exact procedures
___ Critical thinking
___ Logical analysis

___ SUBTOTAL GROUP 1

___ High contact with strangers
___ Actively inspire a variety of people
___ Persuade others to do what needs to be done
___ Generate enthusiasm
___ Sell self & ideas
___ Verbal mastery/ charm

___ SUBTOTAL GROUP 4

Rank

___ Persistence in doing methodical work
___ Patient in following specific instructions
___ Stay at one work station
___ Consistently follow an established pattern
___ Cooperate in assisting others
___ Repetitive work

___ SUBTOTAL GROUP 2

___ Take an idea & move with it
___ Firmness in making decisions
___ Directness in overcoming objections
___ Original thinking
___ Act decisively without precedent
___ Focus on immediate accomplishments

___ SUBTOTAL GROUP 3

Scoring "My Current Job" Profile

Just as you were able to profile yourself in terms of behavioral characteristics so you have just profiled your current or most recent job in terms of job behavior that relate to the four DISC styles. Take a look at the number you have placed in each of the "total" sections of the profile. Which of your groups has the highest subtotal? Write your Group number here:

_____

Group "1" in the upper left corner of the page contains "Compliant" job characteristics, Group "2" in the upper right corner contains "Steady" job characteristics, Group "3" in the lower right corner contains "Director" job characteristics, and Group "4" in the lower left corner contains "Influencer" job characteristics. Right now RANK IN DESCENDING ORDER the four Groups from highest to lowest in terms of the subtotals and next to each place the corresponding DISC letter.

My current (or most recent) job has the following profile:

	Group Number	DISC Letter
Highest job style	_____	_____
Next highest job style	_____	_____
Third highest job style	_____	_____
Lowest job style	_____	_____

Now, let's COMPARE your Current Job Profile (found on Page 67) to your Personal Work Style (found on Page 61). Transfer below both your Current Job Style DISC dimensions as well as your Personal Work Style DISC dimensions IN DESCENDING ORDER:

CURRENT JOB PROFILE: PERSONAL WORK STYLE:

__ Highest Job Style   __ Highest Personal
__ Next highest   __ Next highest
__ Third highest   __ Third highest
__ Lowest   __ Lowest

As you compare these two rankings, what do you notice? Does your Current Job Profile rank exactly match your Personal Work Style? If so, you would appear to be "comfortable" in your current job. Is that true? Yes __ No __

OR, is your Current Job Profile the exact opposite of your Personal Work Style? If so, you are quite likely experiencing a great deal of stress in your current job. Is that true? Yes __ No __

OR, are the two profiles different in one or two rankings and similar in the others? If so, you may be facing some pressure, either from others (like your boss!) or from yourself to adapt your behavior on your current job. Is that true?
Yes __ No __

Profiling My "Ideal Job"

Turn now to the next page and complete the exercise of job profiling one more time. This time, however, attempt to identify your "Ideal Job", the job you would love to have, even though you may not be able at the present time to even give a title to it! Follow the same instructions as you did before, but remember to focus on your "Ideal Job", not your current job.

My ideal job is: _____

My "Ideal Job"

Listed below are a number of characteristics applicable to a variety of jobs. Please respond to each and every item listed by ranking its relative importance as you see it to the successful performance of the job YOU WOULD LIKE TO HOLD. Use the following scale to rank each and every item:

1 Not important
2 Low importance
3 High importance
4 Very high importance

Rank

___ Diplomacy & tact
___ Gather detailed information
___ Follow quality standards
___ Adhere to exact procedures
___ Critical thinking
___ Logical analysis

___ SUBTOTAL GROUP 1

Rank

___ Persistence in doing methodical work
___ Patient in following specific instructions
___ Stay at one work station
___ Consistently follow an established pattern
___ Cooperate in assisting others
___ Repetitive work

___ SUBTOTAL GROUP 2

___ High contact with strangers
___ Actively inspire a variety of people
___ Persuade others to do what needs to be done
___ Generate enthusiasm
___ Sell self & ideas
___ Verbal mastery/charm

___ SUBTOTAL GROUP 4

___ Take an idea & move with it
___ Firmness in making decisions
___ Directness in overcoming objections
___ Original thinking
___ Act decisively without precedent
___ Focus on immediate accomplishments

___ SUBTOTAL GROUP 3

Scoring "My Ideal Job" Profile

Repeat the same steps as you did for your current job profile by ranking in descending order and then comparing your "ideal" job rank to your personal work style rank:

My "Ideal Job" has the following profile:

Highest Job Style   _____
Next highest Job Style   _____
Third highest Job Style   _____
Lowest Job Style   _____

Now, indicate once more the four DISC dimensions of your Personal Work Style you completed on Page 61 IN DESCENDING ORDER:

My highest Personal Work Style   _____
My second Personal Work Style   _____
My third Personal Work Style   _____
My lowest Personal Work Style   _____

As you compare these two rankings, what do you notice?

Is your "Ideal Job" exactly aligned to your personal work style? If so, this is probably a definite indication that you should begin to identify the kinds of jobs or careers that are exactly in harmony with your personal style.

OR, is your "Ideal Job" somewhat different from your personal work style? If so, this is probably an indication that you are looking for a job or career that allows you to experience some variation from, some adaptation of, your personal work style.

Chances are that you have not chosen an "ideal" job that is totally opposite in ranking from your personal style. But if you have, BE CAREFUL! You might wind up placing yourself in an extremely stressful situation for which you may not be ready.

Utilize these item-by-item job characteristics in THINKING THROUGH and, when on an interview, in ASKING ABOUT the job for which you have applied. This will help you focus more precisely and more specifically on what we have referred to in Chapter 2 as "Intangible Tangibles" when trying to decide whether or not to accept a job offer.

We must first cultivate our garden.

-from *Candide* by Voltaire

Chapter 6 Assessing & Profiling Your Skills

Your next challenge is that of assessing and profiling your skills. Identifying the skills necessary for success both in your current and "ideal" jobs is an important first step in the process. The second step is to identify the skills you need to develop in order to be able to be more productive on your current job and to obtain and succeed in your "ideal" job. Being able to articulate a number of key work skills gives you the basis for "taking your skills to the second and third level", the third step in being able to fully document your "Skill Set" and then being able to discuss in relevant detail your strengths and weaknesses with an employment interviewer.

What is a skill? A skill is a behavior that you have practiced enough so that you have achieved a certain level of proficiency. Skills, in other words, are HABITS developed by practice. The following catalogue of skills will very likely be an eye-opener to you. Take a look at the Three Skill Areas presented on Page 75. The specific skills listed under each of the three headings are not meant to be all-inclusive, but rather are representative of each of the three skill areas.

The first area consists of *Technical Skills*. These include the specific working knowledge of an industry as well as a particular job within that industry, together with the appropriate terminology and techniques necessary for the successful performance of that specific job. Let's take an example. Carpentry has its own set of knowledge, for instance, "tongue in groove"; and techniques, for instance, the safe use of a power saw. While this area of skills is the most obvious, it must not be overlooked as you begin to identify and document your own "Skill Set".

The second skill area involves *Functional Skills*. These are generic work skills common to most, if not all, work environments. Included here are such skills as the ability to manage your time well, the ability to organize your thoughts, the ability to plan how to accomplish a task, how to actively listen to others, and the like.

The third skill area is probably the most likely to be overlooked, simply because it is so INDIVIDUAL. These are *Personal Skills* which are applicable to a variety of work situations.

However, just because they are personal in nature does not mean that these skills cannot be learned! For instance, "self confidence" is not an inherited trait, but rather is a personal view of yourself. Self confidence consists of specific behaviors such as self affirmation and the ability to control your thoughts and attitudes about yourself, both of which can be learned and practiced so that they become POSITIVE HABITS.

In like manner, "creativity", the ability to find new or unusual meanings or relationships between ordinary ideas or objects, is another skill that can be learned. Since personal skills are some of the most important for your own career growth, be sure to spend time identifying as many of these as you can.

You can start this process of identification by CIRCLING as many of the skills listed on the next page as you feel apply to you.

Key Skill Areas

Technical Skills

These are the skills which are <u>specific</u> to a given industry and to a job or career within that industry. They are categorized as follows:

- Knowledge
- Techniques
- Terminology

Functional Skills

These are <u>generic</u> work skills that are necessary in almost every work environment. They include:

- Planning
- Motivating
- Disciplining
- Budgeting
- Controlling
- Staffing
- Listening
- Negotiating
- Organizing
- Interviewing
- Training
- Setting standards
- Reporting
- Scheduling
- Conflict resolution
- Time management

Personal Skills

There are a number of <u>personal</u> skills which can, indeed must, be <u>adapted</u> to many life situations. They include:

- Creativity
- Introspection
- Self affirmation
- Self discipline
- Desire to learn
- Role modeling

To continue this exercise, write in the space below at least FIFTEEN SKILLS you currently possess. Start with the skills you circled on the previous page.

MY CURRENT SKILLS include:

1. _____
2. _____
3. _____
4. _____
5. _____
6. _____
7. _____
8. _____
9. _____
10. _____
11. _____
12. _____
13. _____
14. _____
15. _____

Strengths and Weaknesses

How are strengths and weaknesses related to skills? It's really quite straightforward. Think of a strength as a skill you possess. Your skills are your strengths.

Weaknesses are a bit more complex. There are three types of weakness. The first type is the "absence of a skill." For example, if you are unable to read, that's a weakness.

The second type of weakness is the "very limited accomplishment" of a skill. For example, if you can write good internal memos but you produce poor reports and business letters, your writing skills are very limited. It is likely that your boss would criticize you for not being able to write better reports and letters, an essential skill for middle and senior management positions. (While writing good internal memos is, in fact, a partial strength, in the WIDER SKILL of "writing" you are really weaker than stronger if you produce poor reports and business letters).

The third type of weakness may surprise you. A weakness can be the "overuse of a strength." For example, making decisions is a strength. But if you make all of the decisions all of the time about everything, that is a weakness. In relating this to your work style, bear in mind that you can overdo any one of your strengths to the point that it becomes a type of weakness.

Below you will find a list of STRENGTHS categorized by work style. Take time right now to review this list and CIRCLE all the strengths that you feel you have, regardless of what style they are under.

Work Style Strengths

DIRECTORS

- Decisive
- Self assured
- Risk taker
- Result oriented
- Direct
- Assertive
- Quick

INFLUENCERS

- Persuasive
- Confident
- People intuitive
- Gregarious
- Enthusiastic
- Generous
- Optimistic

COMPLIANT

- Conscientious
- Precise
- Systematic
- Diplomatic
- Accurate
- Analytical
- Discreet

STEADY

- Persistent
- Patient
- Deliberate
- Cooperative
- Empathetic
- Sincere
- Even tempered

On the next page you will find a list of WEAKNESSES categorized by work style. Take time right now to review this list and CIRCLE all the weaknesses that you feel apply to you, regardless of what style they are under.

Work Style Weaknesses

DIRECTORS

- Impatient
- Oversteps bounds
- Sarcastic
- Inattentive to details
- Resists team approach
- Cannot slow down/relax

INFLUENCERS

- Impulsive
- Inconsistent
- Too emotional
- Disorganized
- Skips over all details
- Overgeneralizes

COMPLIANT

- Overcautious
- Can't accept limitations
- Gets lost in details
- Low tolerance for ambiguity
- Unforgiving
- Slave to rules
- Indecisive

STEADY

- Overdependent
- Complacent
- Stubborn
- Waits for orders
- Non-assertive
- Resists short cuts
- May avoid all risks

Now that you have finished circling items on the previous two lists you have an excellent "starter inventory" to use as you begin the fascinating process of INTEGRATING YOUR STRENGTHS AND WEAKNESSES TOGETHER WITH YOUR LIKES AND DISLIKES. As a preparation for that task use the worksheet on the next page to write each of the strengths and each of the weaknesses you circled on the previous two lists (plus any others which may have come to mind).

MY CURRENT STRENGTHS include...

_____
_____
_____
_____
_____
_____
_____
_____

MY CURRENT WEAKNESSES include...

_____
_____
_____
_____
_____
_____
_____
_____

Defining Your Strengths and Weaknesses in Detail

Now that you understand the differences in skill areas, it's time to begin the process of developing a deeper understanding of your defined skill set. Why? Because it will provide you with tremendous insight into yourself; it will directly impact your job choices; and it will serve as excellent preparation for your interviews. It will also dramatically improve your interview content, BECAUSE YOU WILL BE ABLE TO FULLY DESCRIBE YOUR STRENGTHS AND WEAKNESSES IN CLEAR DETAIL. This is critical, as most interviewees do not answer questions of this type successfully. This has a major impact on the success of the interview as we will see in Chapter 11.

In simple terms, as you see on Page 82, we have "templated" or overlaid Skills above the concepts of Strengths & Weaknesses and Likes & Dislikes. In other words, we're now going to look at all of these concepts together.

Preparing a Multi-Level Definition of Your Strengths & Weaknesses

One of the most powerful insights that you can gain is in preparing the MULTI-LEVEL DEFINITION OF YOUR WEAKNESSES. Most of us shy away from the recognition of our weaknesses because we don't like to deal with negative information about ourselves. Don't make that mistake! EVERYONE HAS WEAKNESSES. To avoid confronting your weaknesses is to avoid change. The added advantage here is that you will be much better prepared to face the task of addressing your weaknesses, whether in your current position or in a job interview.

You should be open to the possibilities that IMPROVEMENT can bring.

The "Template" View of Skills, Strengths & Weaknesses, Likes & Dislikes

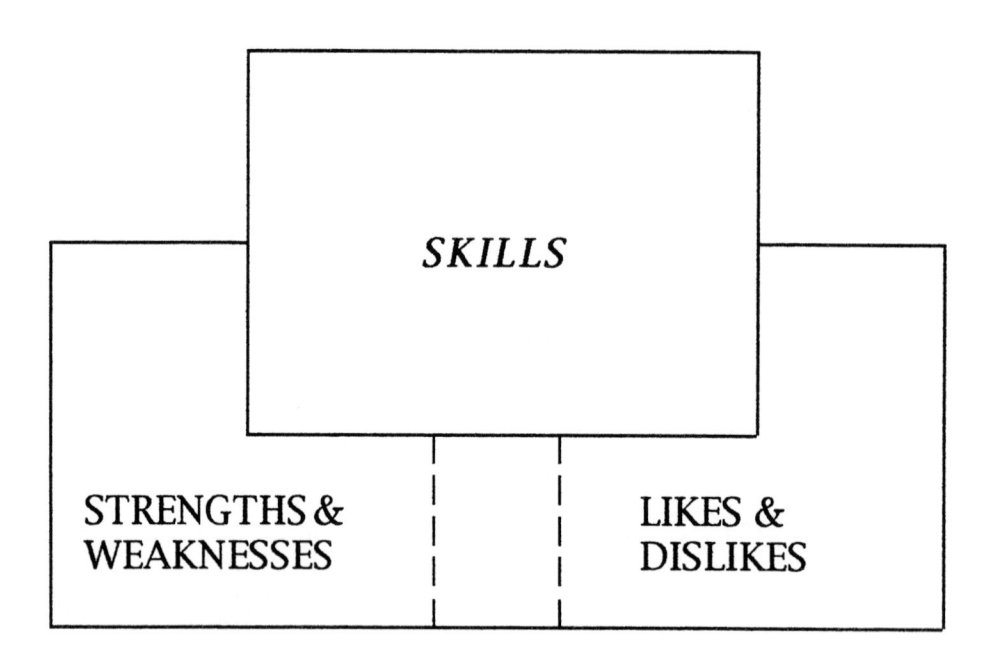

SKILLS

STRENGTHS & WEAKNESSES

LIKES & DISLIKES

Step 1 From your list of Strengths & Weaknesses on Page 80, circle the 5 KEY STRENGTHS and 5 KEY WEAKNESSES you want to examine in greater detail.

Step 2 For each of these, use a separate sheet of paper to prepare a MULTI-LEVEL DEFINITION, going into three levels of increasing detail. Please refer to the completed examples on Pages 84 and 85.

In this definition, you will list the Strength (or Weakness), such as Planning, and describe it in greater detail. Your objective is to describe it in AT LEAST THREE SUCCESSIVELY SPECIFIC LEVELS OF DETAIL. In this way, you will help to clearly define just what comprises each of your major strengths. Don't be afraid to add "environmental" considerations. For example, your Planning strength may be very specific, such as: "I am excellent at planning information systems projects because I provide comprehensive charts regarding time, human resources/staffing and individual assignments. I document these issues in a Planning Report which is prepared and reviewed and then submitted to my supervisor."

Once you have completed your ten multi-level charts, examine them closely to ensure that you have described each strength and weakness in sufficient detail and with accuracy.

Again, refer to the completed examples on Pages 84 and 85.

Example of a Multi-Level Definition of a Strength

STRENGTH:

PLANNING

- Level One

    I am excellent in terms of preparing plans for departmental projects.

- Level Two

    I prepare plans that are both detailed and thorough.

- Level Three

    The plans that I prepare for systems projects are presented in written form, using charts and graphs and entail the projected utilization of staff in terms of their individual components, the hours allotted for completion of each specific task, as well as start and completion dates, and accountability.

Example of a Multi-Level Definition of a Weakness

WEAKNESS:

BUDGETING

- Level One

    I am not particularly strong in preparing my department's operating budget.

- Level Two

    I have been criticized by my boss in terms of level of detail and timeliness of preparation and submission.

- Level Three

    My budget capabilities are limited to the departmental budgets that I prepare quarterly. In terms of preparing other budgets for other departments or the company as a whole, I am not trained in this area and I have not accepted any additional assignments to perform these tasks.

Preparing Your Current Strengths Chart

Since skills are different for everyone, we're going to start by having you QUANTIFY AND CHART your CURRENT STRENGTHS. PLEASE REFER TO PAGES 94, 95, AND 99 AT THIS TIME. NOW, READ THE FOLLOWING INSTRUCTIONS.

Step 1   Prepare Column 1

In this Chart, you see four separate columns. The first column at the left is COLUMN 1. In this column, you will list your five key STRENGTHS in YOUR CURRENT JOB (OR MOST RECENT JOB). Refer to the skills for which you prepared a Multi-Level Definition in the previous section, or refer to the list of SKILLS you identified on Page 76 for helpful hints on skills. An example of a completed chart is shown on Page 95. Let's say, for example, that one of your greatest strengths is PLANNING. You should then list "Planning" in your Current Strengths Chart on Page 94.

It doesn't matter where you place each skill in Column 1. However, try to determine exactly what you mean by PLANNING, before you simply write down the concept. Planning could mean: "making plans to complete a project", OR "planning for budgetary purposes", OR "planning the company's annual outing" or "long range planning". While these activities all involve planning, the techniques and activities involved are VERY DIFFERENT. Try to be as SPECIFIC as possible.

Step 2   Prepare Column 2

Once you have listed your five Strengths, proceed to the next column, Column 2, which asks you to assign a Current Value to each Strength that you have listed. The Current Values are +1 to +5, with +5 representing the Strength that you view AS YOUR STRONGEST and +1 representing the Strength that is lowest (or least strong) among the five strengths that you listed.

If you DECIDE TO list more than five strengths, then you must use more than 5 Current Values. However, USE EACH CURRENT VALUE ONLY ONCE IN YOUR LIST.

Each strength is thus assigned a UNIQUE Current Value which indicates HOW you view its value relative to the other strengths that you have listed.

This is the method we use to QUANTIFY strengths/weaknesses. Please refer to the Graph on Page 98. It describes the system for integrating your Strengths and Weaknesses with your Likes and Dislikes. The horizontal line at the top of the page is a CONTINUUM which carves out the AMOUNT THAT YOU DISLIKE OR LIKE a certain concept. When you list each Strength or Weakness by its assigned "Current Value" (along the vertical line), you will also match it with a specific value (from the horizontal line) indicating how much or how little you like a certain Strength or Weakness. Please refer to the example on Page 99.

Step 3   Prepare Column 3

In Column 3, on the "Current Strengths" Chart on Page 94, you will now assign an L/D COMPONENT to each Strength that you have listed. This represents your measure of how much you LIKE OR DISLIKE a specific STRENGTH that you have listed. While you may use the same L/D value for more than one strength, it is unlikely that you will like or dislike more than one strength the exact same amount; you should try to assign a unique L/D number to each strength.

Preparing Your Current Weaknesses Chart

Once you have completed the chart on Page 94, please do the same for the Chart on Page 96 which lists CURRENT WEAKNESSES. The same instructions apply for the CURRENT WEAKNESSES CHART in terms of its completion, with the exception that weaknesses use negative (-) numbers in Column 2.

Graphing Your Current Strengths and Weaknesses

Once you have completed both Your Current Strengths and Current Weaknesses Charts on Pages 94 and 96, you are ready to graph your CURRENT STRENGTHS AND WEAKNESSES on the graph on Page 98.

BEFORE YOU START, YOU MUST COMPLETE COLUMN 4 FOR THE CHARTS ON PAGES 94 AND 96.

The easiest way to do this is to complete Column 4 on each page. Column 4 is the proper listing of Column 3 and Column 2 components which you will assign to each STRENGTH AND WEAKNESS.

As you now see in Column 2 of both Charts, each Strength and Weakness has an assigned UNIQUE NUMBER combination next to it. Refer to the examples on Pages 95 and 97. Place the numbers of the appropriate chart in Column 4 by following the examples. To do this, you merely find the appropriate combination of components that you assigned in Column 3 and Column 2 in that order. Don't forget that the order is reversed!!!! In other words, LIST YOUR COLUMN 3 COMPONENT FIRST WHEN YOU PREPARE THE COMBINATIONS IN COLUMN 4. AGAIN, REFER TO THE EXAMPLES ON PAGES 95 and 97.

All you have to do now is to place your CURRENT STRENGTHS AND WEAKNESSES ON THE GRAPH using the proper NUMBER COMBINATION. Simply find the appropriate spot on the Graph on Page 98, and place a dot representing that specific combination from Column 4, and write the specific Strength or Weakness next to the dot for identification. IT'S THAT SIMPLE!!

Once you have completed your graph by plotting your Strengths and Weaknesses on the graph, you are ready to review the results. In essence, the points that are on your graph represent a combination of your strengths and weaknesses blended with HOW MUCH YOU LIKE OR DISLIKE THAT SPECIFIC STRENGTH OR WEAKNESS. This is a powerful and extremely useful concept and one which you need to think about in some detail. First of all, it seems unusual to have a STRENGTH which you may NOT LIKE, doesn't it?

An example of this may be balancing your checkbook: You may do it very well, but you may hate doing it! OR you may have described a WEAKNESS that you do LIKE. An example of this may be writing internal memos, which you may not do well but which you love to do! These combinations allow you to view your integrated "skill set" in terms of how satisfied you are in your current job, by carving out the components of what you DO WELL AND WHAT YOU DON'T DO WELL in concert with YOUR LIKES AND DISLIKES — YOUR EMOTIONS.

What's the purpose of this extended exercise? To be able to QUANTIFY IN SPECIFIC TERMS what you do at work. Most people never get to this stage in terms of self knowledge. They convince their inner selves that they know just what their strengths and weaknesses are. In reality, not only do they not know what their true strengths and weaknesses are, but they certainly could not describe them, and MOST IMPORTANTLY, assess them, in any detail.

The ELSON/WRIGHT system allows you to quantify your Strengths and Weaknesses in terms of both your estimated value and your L/D component and to begin to understand in specific terms your level of job satisfaction and whether to consider alternatives.

Charting and Graphing Your Future Strengths and Weaknesses

On Pages 100 and 101, you will see the SIMILAR charts for indicating Strengths and Weaknesses. They are repeated with one exception. In these charts we refer to FUTURE STRENGTHS AND FUTURE WEAKNESSES. These charts allow you to REFLECT on a potential position, whether it is a specific JOB OFFER, TRANSFER OR PROMOTION, and to characterize the position in terms of the specific skills that you will utilize and HOW MUCH YOU WILL ENJOY PERFORMING THEM.

In order for this to be effective, you must be able to PROJECT the specific STRENGTHS AND WEAKNESSES THAT YOU ALREADY HAVE and how these will appear in the FUTURE POSITION. Once you have completed this process, you can then list the FUTURE STRENGTHS AND WEAKNESSES in a similar fashion, and plot them on a separate blank graph as appears on Page 102.

The obvious value of plotting FUTURE STRENGTHS and WEAKNESSES is that it allows you to compare and contrast your CURRENT VALUES WITH THOSE IN THE FUTURE. Projecting Future Strengths and Weaknesses is a little bit like baseball. If you are a good fastball hitter, then you must PROJECT your success for the next game by looking at the pitchers for the opposing team. If they throw a lot of fastballs, the pitch that you hit the best, how will you do?

Can you visualize yourself in the batter's box? Looking deeply at your strengths and weaknesses in relation to a future environment will allow you to VISUALIZE your success and to PROJECT yourself into the position. You should then be able to predict, with some degree of accuracy, just how you will feel in this new position.

In addition, the value of this exercise is that it allows you to take your CURRENT SKILLS and to view them carefully in terms of how much you Like or Dislike each one. Since the environment (or organization's culture, or department's culture, etc.) is different in each workplace, you should project as clearly and as specifically as possible. This means that if you selected PLANNING as your greatest Strength (You valued it as a 5 in Column 2) and the strength that you Liked the Most (You valued it as a 5 in Column 3), then you must understand HOW YOUR NEXT POSITION WILL IMPACT YOUR SKILL OF PLANNING.

USE THE SPACE BELOW TO SELECT A SPECIFIC STRENGTH OR WEAKNESS THAT YOU HAVE CHARTED AND DESCRIBE HOW THE WORK ENVIRONMENT IMPACTS IT. HINT: Consider the type of planning that is required, the timeframes that are allotted, the individual members of your work team and the organization's culture.

_____

_____

_____

_____

_____

_____

_____

_____

USE THE SPACE BELOW TO PROJECT HOW A SPECIFIC FUTURE ENVIRONMENT WILL IMPACT YOUR CHOSEN STRENGTH OR WEAKNESS:

_____
_____
_____
_____
_____
_____
_____
_____
_____

Summary

The power of this exercise is in your ability to take the time to properly assess your "skill set" and to review it in relation to how much you enjoy a particular activity. Then you can either plot another graph for a FUTURE position or use the information to gain greater insight into your "skill set". Once you have the opportunity to take on new responsibilities or a new job, you can refer to the chart and determine just how the job "stacks up" in comparison to your current inventory of most important skills.

This will allow you to refine your approach, to suggest ways that the organization can flex to support you, to identify areas in which you need specific training, or to plan specific discussions with your boss or work team.

THE RESULT WILL BE A DRAMATICALLY CLEARER PICTURE OF YOUR SKILLS AND AN APPROACH WHICH YOU CAN USE FOR ON-GOING SELF-EVALUATION.

If you care to take the exercise one final step, respond below by stating exactly how you are going to improve upon each weakness that you described in your own chart on Page 96. In this way, you'll be headed straight towards our next Chapter—PROACTIVITY.

Steps I Will Take to Improve My Weaknesses

LIST EACH WEAKNESS FOLLOWED BY A SPECIFIC PLAN TO IMPROVE EACH ONE:

_____
_____
_____
_____
_____
_____
_____
_____
_____
_____

Current Strengths

COLUMN 1	COLUMN 2	COLUMN 3	COLUMN 4
STRENGTH	STRENGTH CURRENT VALUE	L/D COMPONENT	(L/D, STRENGTH)
	(+1 to +5; +5 is highest. Use each number only once. Value must be positive).	(Assign a value of -5 to +5 which represents your level of like or dislike for each strength).	

Example of a Completed Current Strengths Chart

Current Strengths

COLUMN 1	COLUMN 2	COLUMN 3	COLUMN 4
STRENGTH	STRENGTH CURRENT VALUE (+1 to +5; +5 is highest. Use each number only once. Value must be positive).	L/D COMPONENT (Assign a value of -5 to +5 which represents your level of like or dislike for each strength).	(L/D, STRENGTH)
PLANNING	+3	+2	(+2,+3)
CREATIVITY	+2	+4	(+4,+2)
LISTENING	+1	+3	(+3,+1)
PREPARING ACCOUNTING STATEMENTS	+5	-2	(-2,+5)
PROJECT STAFFING	+4	-3	(-3,+4)

Current Weaknesses

COLUMN 1	COLUMN 2	COLUMN 3	COLUMN 4
WEAKNESS	WEAKNESS	L/D COMPONENT	(L/D, WEAKNESS)
	CURRENT VALUE		
	(-1 to -5; -5 is highest. Use each number only once. Value must be -).	(Assign a value of -5 to +5 which represents your level of like or dislike for each weakness).	

Example of a Completed Current Weaknesses Chart

Current Weaknesses

COLUMN 1	COLUMN 2	COLUMN 3	COLUMN 4
WEAKNESS	WEAKNESS CURRENT VALUE (-1 to -5; -5 is highest. Use each number only once. Value must be -).	L/D COMPONENT (Assign a value of -5 to +5 which represents your level of like or dislike for each weakness).	(L/D, WEAKNESS)
BUDGETING	-3	+3	(+3,-3)
CONFLICT RESOLUTION	-2	-2	(-2,-2)
PREPARING TIME REPORTS	-1	-4	(-4,-1)
INCOME TAX PREPARATION	-5	+3	(+3,-5)
MOTIVATING EMPLOYEES	-4	+5	(+5,-4)

Integrating Your Current Strengths/Weaknesses and Likes/Dislikes

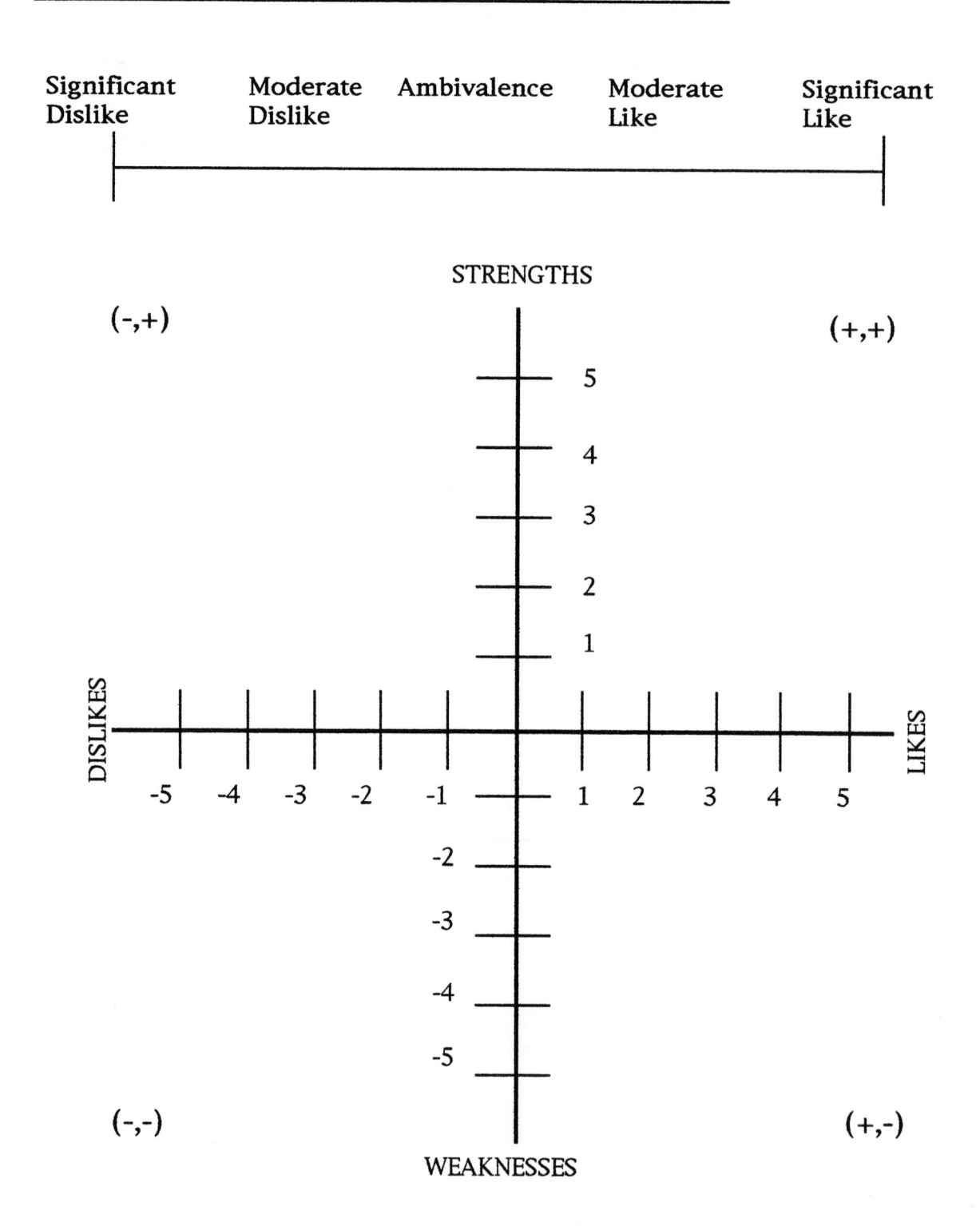

Significant Dislike — Moderate Dislike — Ambivalence — Moderate Like — Significant Like

STRENGTHS

(-,+)   (+,+)

5
4
3
2
1

DISLIKES -5 -4 -3 -2 -1   1   2   3   4   5 LIKES

-2
-3
-4
-5

(-,-)   (+,-)

WEAKNESSES

Example of a Completed Graph

Integrating Your Current Strengths/Weaknesses and Likes/Dislikes

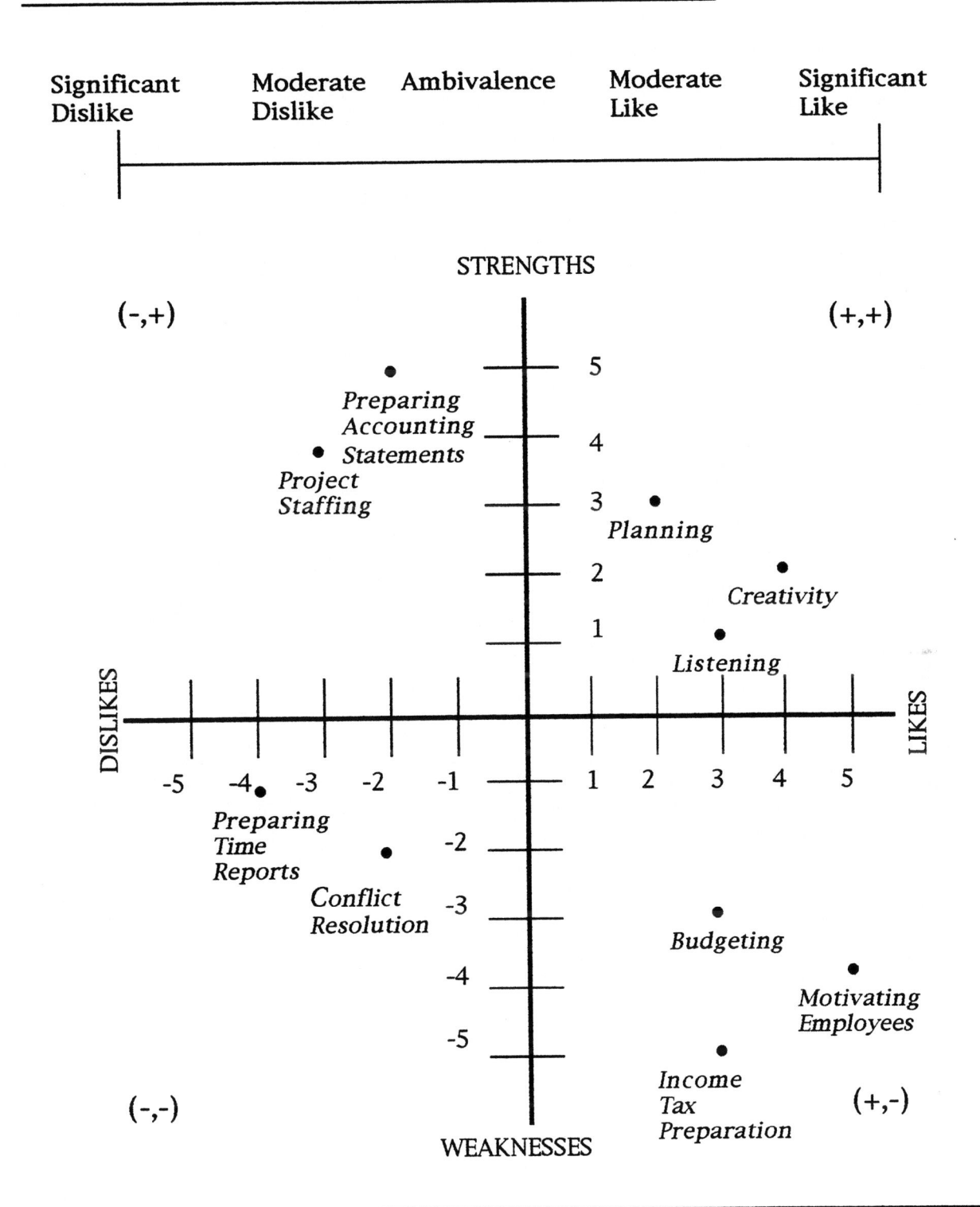

Significant Dislike — Moderate Dislike — Ambivalence — Moderate Like — Significant Like

STRENGTHS

(−,+) (+,+)

- Preparing Accounting Statements (−2, 5)
- Project Staffing (−3, 4)
- Planning (2, 3)
- Creativity (4, 2)
- Listening (3, 1)

DISLIKES ←→ LIKES

- Preparing Time Reports (−4, −1)
- Conflict Resolution (−2, −2)
- Budgeting (3, −3)
- Motivating Employees (5, −4)
- Income Tax Preparation (3, −5)

(−,−) (+,−)

WEAKNESSES

99

Future Strengths

COLUMN 1	COLUMN 2	COLUMN 3	COLUMN 4
STRENGTH	STRENGTH FUTURE VALUE	L/D COMPONENT	(L/D, STRENGTH)
	(+1 to +5; +5 is highest. Use each number only once. Value must be positive).	(Assign a value of -5 to +5 which represents your level of like or dislike for each strength).	

Future Weaknesses

COLUMN 1	COLUMN 2	COLUMN 3	COLUMN 4
WEAKNESS	WEAKNESS FUTURE VALUE	L/D COMPONENT	(L/D, WEAKNESS)
	(-1 to -5; -5 is highest. Use each number only once. Value must be -).	(Assign a value of -5 to +5 which represents your level of like or dislike for each weakness).	

Integrating Your Future Strengths/ Weaknesses and Likes/Dislikes

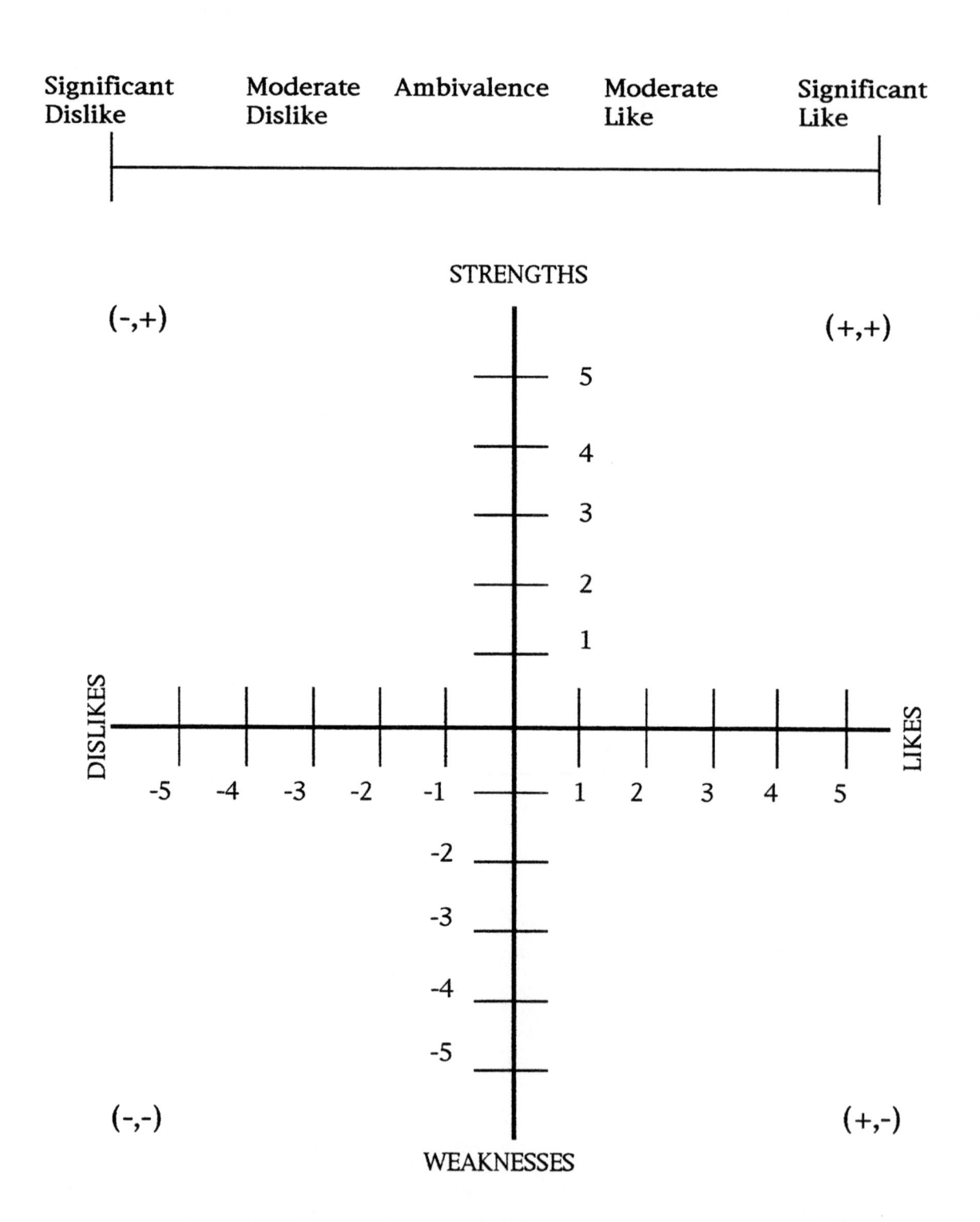

Significant Dislike — Moderate Dislike — Ambivalence — Moderate Like — Significant Like

STRENGTHS

(-,+)　　　　　　　　　　　　　　　　(+,+)

5
4
3
2
1

DISLIKES　-5 -4 -3 -2 -1 | 1 2 3 4 5　LIKES

-2
-3
-4
-5

(-,-)　　　　　　　　　　　　　　　　(+,-)

WEAKNESSES

The Personal Marketing Dimension

Luck is when preparation meets opportunity.

-John Wooden

Chapter 7 Proactivity

The value of personal career development is that it will provide you with the tools necessary to expand your horizons. In this sense, it is a process, a way of thinking, a way of life. One of the most significant components of personal career development is PROACTIVITY. As we discussed in Chapter 1, proactivity is "The initiation of thoughts, plans, and activities by an individual based on his/her personal motivation". The ability to proactively manage your career is essential in today's job market. The tools of the past, INCLUDING responding to ads in the paper or waiting for the executive recruiter (or headhunter) to call, are, in general, only partially productive and have a great deal to do with LUCK. WHY LEAVE YOUR CAREER TO CHANCE? Proactivity provides much more predictable results and helps your ego strengthen itself by providing a positive channel for your energy.

What Comprises Proactivity?

In terms of our discussion, proactivity involves two activities:

- The identification of the positive factors in a job environment which maximize your performance and elicit the most positive response from you;

- The initiation of activities that will propel you toward finding a position with these characteristics.

Both concepts are important to your ultimate career success. By identifying the positive factors first, and by following through with the other aspects of this workbook, you will be well-prepared to SEEK OUT THE SPECIFIC ENVIRONMENT WHICH IS BEST FOR YOU.

A large percentage of individuals that we counsel, either in our seminars or individually, are caught in the same dilemma: EACH ONE WANTS TO FIND A BETTER POSITION WITHIN HIS/HER CURRENT COMPANY, TO CHANGE COMPANIES OR TO CHANGE CAREERS. Yet, most individuals feel trapped by the SPECIFICITY of today's job market. If you are one of these people, this probably means that you don't know how to change from one type of position to another. We have found that this is primarily because people today have convinced themselves that the job market WILL NOT ALLOW THEM TO CHANGE. This is an example of reactive thinking.

A much better way to approach the problem is to continue to define WHO YOU ARE and WHAT MAKES YOU TICK so that you can GO DIRECTLY TO THE JOB MARKET WITH A CLEAR IDEA OF YOUR SELF AND THEREBY FIND THE BEST SITUATION FOR YOU.

A Practical Job Search Approach

In order to be successful in managing your career, you need to take control just as you would with any other important business project. Unfortunately, WHEN IT COMES TO FINDING A BETTER POSITION, most of us don't view our careers as something that can be managed. This is because we tend to believe that:

- If we work hard and pay our dues, everything will fall into place;

- If we are employed by a reputable organization and commit ourselves to moving up the ladder that we are assured of career success and more importantly, contentment;
- If we find the perfect mentor, he/she will take care of us no matter what happens to the company;
- If all else fails we can take a position on an interim basis or work "as a consultant".

While there will always be individuals for whom these rationales ultimately work out, it is far "safer", smarter and more sensible to be well-prepared and self-directed.

The Human Mind

The human mind is an exceptionally complex and powerful machine. It allows us to accomplish a multitude of tasks, to remember ideas and concepts from a variety of unrelated areas, and to control our actions. Therein lies the rub.

For most of us, OUR MIND CONTROLS US.

Because we need to understand how to CONTROL IT, it is important to relate to the mind on a practical basis. The human mind is made up of about 100 billion nerve cells, each of which is composed of thousands of connections. The cells and linkages undergo constant change.

In psychological terms, the mind is composed of the Id (or instinctual impulses), the Ego (or self, also that section which is conscious), and the Superego (or the unconscious section, including the conscience). In more practical terms, our mind contains conscious and subconscious components. The subconscious mind exerts influence over us in subtle ways.

In his book, EMOTIONS OF NORMAL PEOPLE, William Moulton Marston discusses the study of human behavior on a two-axis model according to an individual's action in a favorable or unfavorable environment. The subconscious mind contributes heavily in pushing the individual away from environments which are difficult or distasteful and in propelling the individual towards situations which are pleasurable. The subconscious mind achieves this by retaining near its surface the feelings that are elicited from certain sensory-laden situations. For instance, when you are a child, you learn to stay away from hot surfaces because you are taught, either by an adult, or through personal experience, that you will be burned if you get too close.

Enough PAINFUL experiences of this type pattern your behavior so that your subconscious mind will propel you away from extreme heat EVEN WHEN YOUR CONSCIOUS MIND IS NOT FULLY FOCUSED ON THE SOURCE. Over time we learn or pattern our behavior through our past experience.

Since all environments fit somewhere on the continuum between unfavorable and favorable, it stands to reason that many individuals choose their jobs through reactivity or movement AWAY from something that is unfavorable.

They know and FEEL very clearly about the "factors" in their current job which they don't like, but they are often unsure about what "factors" they do enjoy.

In terms of career development this is a very risky approach. It forces you to approach a position change or the job market with the belief that you must MINIMIZE THE NEGATIVE VS. MAXIMIZING THE POSITIVE.

LIST BELOW THE FEELINGS, SITUATIONS AND INTERACTIONS THAT ELICIT THE MOST NEGATIVE RESPONSE FROM YOU IN YOUR CURRENT OR MOST RECENT WORK ENVIRONMENT:

_____

_____

_____

_____

_____

_____

NOW, LOOK CLOSELY AT THESE NEGATIVE "FACTORS". ARE THERE SPECIFIC ONES WHICH YOU HAVE IDENTIFIED THAT HAVE EXISTED IN OTHER WORK ENVIRONMENTS?

_____

_____

_____

_____

_____

_____

_____

_____

Obviously, recognition of what you don't like IS IMPORTANT. It will help you to recognize situations and environments that elicit negative feelings. The key is to use these negatives to HELP YOU FORMULATE A VIEW OF THE POSITIVE.

As you have seen in previous chapters, you also need to clearly understand what it is that YOU LIKE, AND TO TAKE STEPS TOWARD FINDING A POSITION THAT CONTAINS THESE COMPONENTS in order to make an effective, informed change.

Moving away from, or reacting to, a negative work environment may provide significant insight into the best situation for you. However, IT MUST BE COUPLED WITH AN UNDERSTANDING OF WHAT ATTRACTS YOU in order to be truly effective.

While it is true that some individuals have used reactivity as a major component of their approach, for most of us the current job market is far too volatile, too unpredictable, and certainly too competitive to follow this singular approach.

NOW, LIST BELOW THE FEELINGS, SITUATIONS AND INTERACTIONS THAT ELICIT THE MOST POSITIVE RESPONSE FROM YOU IN YOUR CURRENT WORK ENVIRONMENT:

_____

_____

_____

_____

_____

_____

_____

_____

NOW, LOOK CLOSELY AT THESE POSITIVE "FACTORS". ARE THERE SPECIFIC ONES WHICH YOU HAVE IDENTIFIED THAT HAVE EXISTED IN OTHER WORK ENVIRONMENTS?

_____
_____
_____
_____
_____
_____
_____
_____
_____

Applying Your Personal Knowledge

What is required TODAY is a combined approach which starts with A SHIFT IN ATTITUDE. One of the clearest concepts in THE PERSONAL MARKETING DIMENSION is the idea that proactivity generates more direct, focused and generally faster results in seeking a new position than does reactivity.

Why this occurs is very clear:

- Once you have identified the environmental factors that elicit the best response from you, you can gear your job search towards the maximization of these factors;

- Proactivity pushes you into the job market, versus your sitting back and waiting for the job market to come to you;

- Proactivity allows you to define and refine EXACTLY what you are seeking in terms of a position, versus accepting whatever is presented to you;

- Proactivity affords you with significant "mental power" and increased self confidence because it provides your psyche with the higher energy that comes from taking control of your destiny;

- In short, PROACTIVITY PUTS YOU IN CONTROL!

NOW, LIST AT LEAST FIVE TASKS THAT DESCRIBE YOUR VIEW OF WHAT IS REQUIRED TO SECURE A NEW POSITION IN TODAY'S MARKETPLACE:

_____

_____

_____

_____

_____

What did you list? In order to be successful in this marketplace, you need to initiate a plan which includes at least the following components:

- Development of a comprehensive list of potential employers based on preferences in industry, company size, location, potential FOR YOU to be hired in the right function, at the right level (we have included an initial research list in the back of the book);

- Construction of a Job Search Log which includes the Contact Name, Company Name, Date of Contact and Status for each prospective employer. See the next section.

The Job Search Log

The Job Search Log is most easily constructed in a three-ring binder with alphabetical dividers separating each section. Use the Contact Name or Company Name as your alpha guide and place a standard page within the section with the following information listed in columns:

- CONTACT NAME
- COMPANY NAME
- DATE OF CONTACT
- TYPE OF CONTACT
- STATUS

Once the Job Search Log is in place, you should attach (in the appropriate section) all correspondence that you have sent to the company, or that has been sent to you, so that it is easily found in the proper section.

In addition, a Proactive Job Search should include:

- Networking within your specific arena through industry and trade associations, industry and trade publications, seminars, and contact with individuals that serve specific industries such as lawyers, consultants and accountants;

- A willingness to work FULL-TIME to achieve your end result. This means that you must realize that it doesn't matter HOW MANY REJECTIONS YOU RECEIVE BECAUSE YOU NEED ONLY ONE POSITION.

- Pulling out all the stops, including making contact with publication editors and writers and identifying key players within specific groups of interest. THE OBJECTIVE HERE IS TO SEEK REFERRALS TO OTHERS THAT MAY BE IN A POSITION TO HIRE YOU.

- Identify 5 key people that you know. Ask each one to provide just two names of individuals they know that might help you. If they will call the individuals in advance and let them know you'll be calling them — so much the better. At least, ask permission to use their name when you call the individuals. You'll quickly have 10 additional contacts!

- Establish a program of regular training, encompassing both your current areas of interest and your future plans. This should include enough exposure to personal computers that you become comfortable using the "current software." THIS APPROACH WILL HELP TO ENSURE THAT YOU NEVER STOP LEARNING AND GROWING.

Finally, you should understand that it takes years to become truly well-versed in terms of adding a skill, a behavior or a new image to your inventory. In Chapters 11 and 12, we provide useful ideas as to how this can be most easily achieved.

Everyone excels in something in which another fails.

-Publilius Syrus

Chapter 8　Developing Your Resume and Cover Letter

Overview

There are many books available on the subject of resumes. Our purpose here is not to duplicate what is already written, nor to stop you from choosing a book to read. We simply want to provide some insight into WHAT MAKES A RESUME AND COVER LETTER SUCCESSFUL.

Although there are many different types of resumes, by far the most popular and easiest to read is the Chronological Resume, which lists work experience from most current to least current. The advantage is that the present position, or most recent position is stated first. Since your most current experience will be viewed as the most direct for your next position, we believe that it is best to list it first.

It is also important to provide comprehensive dates of employment, such as 1972 to 1979, as it presents a straightforward image. Individuals that choose not to use actual dates of employment, or that decide to use a Summary Form of resume should realize that they are providing the reader with a reason to be circumspect about the information presented. The more factual, straightforward and honest your presentation, the more likely the reader will NOT be asking herself/himself "what is this person hiding"? The same issue applies to other types of resumes.

Since we will not cover resumes other than chronological resumes in this chapter, please feel free to pick up a book on resume writing from your local library or bookstore should you decide to write something other than a Chronological Resume.

Components of the Successful Resume

A successful cover letter and resume campaign begins with self-knowledge. The exercises that you have completed in Chapters 1 through 7 will help dramatically. Once you have established reasonable self-knowledge, it is easiest to begin developing your resume by completing a SKELETON such as the one that appears on Pages 135 and 136. By completing this skeleton, you'll be ready to write your resume and have it finished in a very short period of time.

Before you start the process of completing the skeleton, LET'S REVIEW THE COMPONENTS OF A SUCCESSFUL RESUME:

- A resume is a summation of your work experience, education, accomplishments and perhaps, your civic activities. Some people like to include a limited amount of personal information such as hobbies, outside interests, etc. Other people include marital status, height, weight and age.

  The latter is not necessary for a successful resume, but you may include it if you feel your situation warrants disclosure of this information up front. Furthermore, you need not include actual Business References in the body of the resume — they are better placed on a separate sheet which you may attach to the resume if you so desire. That way, they can be modified without impacting the entire resume. Personal references, such as friends or family members are becoming less and less accepted in the business world. The reason for this is clear: most individuals provide personal references that will speak favorably about the person. In this respect, when a potential employer (or the agent of the employer) calls to solicit commentary on the person, the information that is provided is generally positive and consistent from one source to another. Therefore, it has minimal value in determining a candidate's qualifications for employment.

Most resumes have a statement such as "REFERENCES AVAILABLE UPON REQUEST". This is standard terminology indicating to the reader that you have a list of references that you will make available at the proper time. When you do provide this information, make sure that you have cleared this with each specific reference.

You should never assume that another person will serve as a business reference for you regardless of your perception of your association with that person. In addition, if you are aware that a potential employer will be calling your references in the near future, it is common courtesy to notify your reference of this fact. In this way, you will also minimize the amount of "telephone tag" between your reference and the caller.

- A resume has one purpose — to get you an interview. Remember this point when you are writing, as many people write their resume as if they ARE describing their entire life on one or two sheets of paper. This approach ends up creating a document which is too detailed, cluttered and difficult to read. Incidentally, we believe that in almost every circumstance A RESUME SHOULD BE NO LONGER THAN ONE OR TWO PAGES.

Our rationale for this is clear. The vast majority of individuals that will be reviewing your resume are very busy. They include presidents, functional executives, human resources professionals, recruiters, headhunters and executive search professionals (those that work on retainer for specific client companies).

Not only do they have many responsiblities besides reviewing resumes, but they receive large amounts of resumes on an on-going basis.

YOUR RESUME MUST CONVINCE THESE BUSY READERS OF YOUR VALUE WITHIN A FEW MINUTES OF THEIR FIRST READING.

These individuals are most likely to read your resume if:

- It is well-organized;
- Factual;
- Contains plenty of "white space" (or open areas that make it easier to read); and
- Describes the highlights of your career and education briefly and clearly.

In general, when it comes to resume writing: LESS IS MORE. After all, if you provide too much information, describing everything about a given experience, it reduces the reader's incentive to invite you in for a personal meeting. And don't forget, it's the personal meeting that gets you the job, not the resume. THE RESUME MERELY OPENS THE DOOR.

Let's look specifically at a few different resumes. On the following pages you will see several examples of actual resumes. All references to individual names and company names have been deleted to maintain confidentiality.

Critique of Sample Resume #1

On Pages 124-126, you'll see Sample Resume #1. This first resume is an example of a person with good intention and poor execution. While it is important in a resume to provide plenty of quantifiable information, such as the size of your department, budget, sales volume, etc., this person has gone way overboard.

The key here is that this resume is too long, far too EXPANSIVE in descriptive phrases and is very cluttered. It does not give the reader a lot of incentive to read the material. THIS IS A CRITICAL POINT: WRITE YOUR RESUME FROM THE READER'S STANDPOINT.

ASK YOURSELF THE FOLLOWING QUESTIONS BEFORE YOU START YOUR FIRST DRAFT:

- Is all the information that I have summarized really important?

- Is the information factual and does it accurately represent each situation that is described?

- Have I included the actual dates of employment for each position represented?

- Is there enough information to provide a clear picture as to my level of professional and technical competence in my field of expertise?

- Have I included information about POSITIONS OF RESPONSIBILITY in civic, educational and work situations?

- Have I included enough information about my employer companies to provide the reader with insight into the size, type of business, and location?

If you can answer YES to all of these questions, the chances are quite good that your resume will contain the appropriate level of detail. Don't forget that people like to hire LEADERS. Anything that you can provide which indicates your level of leadership (as well as accomplishment) is in your favor.

Critique of Sample Resume #2

Now, let's quickly review the second resume. The second resume is a lot easier to read than the first, especially in terms of organization. The Professional Experience is summarized in chronological order, the titles of each position are clearly labelled, and the activities are summarized underneath. The resume could improve by using bullet points instead of paragraphs.

This requires a shorter synopsis of each point mentioned and will help keep the resume from being overly wordy. In addition, the resume could benefit from dates in the education section as well as more specific information. The use of the statement "Numerous seminars and additional courses" is far too general.

Critique of Sample Resume #3

Sample Resume #3 is an example of a combined approach where the first page summarizes achievements and the second page provides the chronological data. We view this as confusing and unnecessary. It forces the reader to guess which achievements fit with which position, even if they are shown in parentheses. Again, remember to write your resume as though YOU will be reading it.

A concise well-written two-page synopsis of experience will provide the reader with a clear statement of who you are and what you have accomplished. The reader can then easily glean the details from the resume. When there is plenty of white space, the descriptions are brief, yet complete, and the dates and facts correspond to one another. In short, the resume is well-organized, complete and pleasing to read. Take a look at the resume entitled SAMPLE RESUME #4. This resume is straightforward, yet comprehensive. It has all the components that we have described.

If you are a college student, look at Sample Resumes #5 and #6 on Pages 133-134. The first could be improved by being less wordy and using bullet format. The second is probably too brief.

Prepare Your Skeleton Resume

NOW, LET'S BEGIN YOUR PREPARATION OF THE SKELETON RESUME ON PAGES 135 and 136. First, complete the information at the top of the resume. Next, if you choose to use an objective, make sure that it is as specific as possible. For example, "To secure the position of General Manager in a multi-plant manufacturing company that produces health and beauty aid products." Ambiguous objectives serve no valuable purpose. Next, complete the sections regarding experience. Include dates, titles, location of the company, a brief description of the company (or division) and both your responsibilities and accomplishments.

Finally, complete the Education Section, including dates, the specific degree, location and other information. Fill in Personal and Interest information, if you desire, and add a statement regarding the availability of references, such as the one found at the bottom of the page.

SAMPLE RESUME #1

December
- Present

Vice President - Operations

Recruited to this $65 million division of $450 million NYSE corporation by then President   when sales were just under $47 million to take full responsibility for manufacturing of   broad line of emergency signalling devices.

            was faced with very large and unfavorable start-up costs associated with a recently completed plant relocation and the implementation of revised processes at the new location aimed at supporting very large sales growth projections. I was charged with "fixing manufacturing" and given total authority to implement corrective measures. Although the sales growth never materialized, I have successfully transformed the organization into a strong customer orientation through the application of World Class Manufacturing concepts.   Division enjoys the market leader position in quality, delivery, price and innovation. With this success, I'm seeking a new challenge.. hopefully a Presidency; otherwise Chief Operations Officer with early transition to general management, in an organization which seeks to become a World Class Organization.

Following (with the permission of   the current division President) is a summary of the division's performance since I joined in December 1983:

	Sales (millions)	ROI %	Employees Mfg/Total	Manufacturing Expense (millions)	% Sales	Inventory (millions)
19	$64.2	20.9	313/526	$11.7	18.4	$ 9.6
19	$62.7	16.2	345/553	$12.7	20.2	$11.6
19	$65.1	12.3	402/612	$12.7	19.5	$15.2
19	$64.4	9.4	462/696	$13.7	21.2	$18.2
19	$61.8	4.5	535/768	$14.0	22.8	$18.8
19	$59.5	8.2	527/779	$14.4	24.2	$17.2
19	$57.3	5.3	494/770	$14.1	24.6	$18.8
19	$46.9	1.0	513/765	$12.9	27.4	$19.8

Long term strategic planning in 1986 recognized that the division had lost its customer orientation. In early 1987 Strategic Business Units (SBUs) were formed in the sales and marketing functions and engineering for new product development transferred later that same year. The large centralized manufacturing organization under my direction has taken a World Class Manufacturing strategy as the most logical and effective route to develop the SBUs as stand-alone businesses. In early 1991, we are completing a plant rearrangement which will reduce floor space requirements from present 420,000 square feet by over 35%, which will be leased-out at an annual rate of over $500,000, which falls right to the bottom line. All SBUs are enjoying significant improvement in throughput cycle time and most are at an on-time delivery to customer promise date of over 95%. Cost of Quality for 1990 was under 1.5% of sales, down from over 5% in 1983. Negotiated several large concessionary agreements with the four bargaining units at   Division.

SAMPLE RESUME #1, PAGE 2

Processes in place at   include: assembly of electronic and electro-mechanical equipment, several microprocessor based; sheet metal and machine shops (CNC and conventional punching presses, NC lathes and chuckers, drilling and tapping); tool and die manufacturing; wire and cable harness manufacturing; fully automatic electrostatic painting; printed circuit board assembly with ATE testing.

June   <u>Vice President Operations.</u> Promoted in title with additional responsibilities of R&D, MIS and CAD, Quality Assurance, and Design Engineering. In addition I presently am part of the Executive Committee which oversees the SBU organizations and the Strategic Planning process. Also Office Services and Payroll were added in

Dec.   <u>Vice President Manufacturing.</u> Joined   Division in charge of manufacturing, facility management, materials management which included purchasing, production control, traffic and warehousing, and manufacturing engineering reporting to the President.

May
 -December

Joined this world leading producer of
            directly from college. This privately held company's sales in   were approximately $100 million as compared to just under $30 million in 19 . Enjoyed several levels of engineering and manufacturing responsibility which afforded me an accelerated education in operations management.

   19   <u>Director - Central Manufacturing Engineering</u>

        Promoted and returned to   main manufacturing facility in   , to take corporation-wide responsibility for mechanical, industrial, plant, and tool engineering as well as advanced technologies serving seven manufacturing locations nationwide. Reporting to the Vice President of Operations Services, my staff of twenty professionals was actively pursuing cost reduction techniques and the implementation of an MRP-II strategy adopted by the company. Projects undertaken included justification of robotics   polishing line and the automation of deep draw hydraulic presses. Developed and managed capital budget in excess of $5 million.

   19   <u>Plant Manager</u>

        Promoted and given full responsibility for   manufacturing plant in   , in an effort to turn around a floundering operation. The plant was strategically located to supply low cost high volume   to the western United States, Canada, and Mexico under several brand names. Sales grew from $2 million to $5 million during my tenure. I successfully brought back profitability to the   through improved labor efficiency, lower indirect labor and scrap, reduction of freight-out costs by over 50%, and achievement of lowest packaging costs in the industry through innovative design and negotiation with suppliers. Successfully negotiated two collective bargaining agreements while downsizing the organization from 100 to 40 over my five year stay.

19   **Supervisor - Industrial Engineering Group**

Promoted over more senior employees to be   first engineering supervisor within the Manufacturing Engineering organization at the   main plant. Major projects included the start-up of a   manufacturing division, the consolidation of two divisions after an acquisition from   Corporation, expansion of three   manufacturing plants, and the design and implementation of an over $1 million main plant modernization. Processes included deep draw, heat treating, automated polishing and grinding, refrigeration systems, welding and brazing, painting, and electrical assembly.

19   **Manufacturing Engineer**

Joined   out of college as Junior Industrial Engineer and quickly was retitled to Manufacturing Engineer in recognition of the immediate contributions being made to the organization. Major projects included MTM standards development for four plants, start-up of new venture   operation and later relocation to new manufacturing facility in   . Position afforded me broad experience in all aspects of process and production supervision and became the foundation for much of my later success in dealing with production floor problems.

Prior 19   Various jobs while pursuing formal education including packing house worker and union member, night manager for fast food restaurant, manager of rock band, house manager for fraternity, and founding partner in a successful campus photographic service.

EDUCATION: BS-Industrial Engineering, University of Illinois, 19
             MBA-Marketing, DePaul University, 19

I have developed and conduct for my employees on a regular basis a college equivalent course in Operations Management and World Class Manufacturing based upon the teachings of Richard Schonberger and W. Edwards Deming as well as the American Management Association. This is my way of giving something back for the education and training that I have received. I hope to continue this activity in my next position as it has greatly contributed to my personal satisfaction and business successes.

PERSONAL: Born
            Married, no children.

SAMPLE RESUME #2

SUMMARY

Highly experienced in Engineering and Marketing Management, involving a great variety of products generally electromechanical, electronic, and lighting components for the transportation industry.

PROFESSIONAL EXPERIENCE

CORPORATION.   2/   to Present

NEW TECHNOLOGIES MANAGER   (10   to Present)

Responsible for coordinating transfer of technology from sister divisions into the automotive market.   Group includes ten divisions with expertise ranging from micromachining to position sensing and temperature sensing, along with various other technologies. The development of synergism within the Group is expected to lead to expanded opportunities with the Division's individual markets and, in particular, to increased diversification and sales to the transportation industry for the   . Division.

PRODUCT ENGINEERING MANAGER   (2/   to 9/)

Directed engineering activities on components such as circuit breakers, pressure switches, solenoids, electronic assemblies, and many other products supplied to the transportation industry. Products are used in applications such as engine and transmission control, braking systems, comfort and convenience, and controls/instrumentation. The Product Engineering Department staff of 45 employees, one third professional, includes very good support facilities in the areas of Model Shop, Test Labs, Vehicle Lab, and CAD equipment.

1/82 to 1/87

DIRECTOR OF ENGINEERING

         is owned by ,   based   a large, worldwide electrical component supplier to the transportation industry.   includes   , manufacturer of automated) and electronic control devices; and   a joint venture company with two   manufacturers.   include   devices. Customers included the Big Three, AMC, VWOA, BMW, several Japanese transplants, heavy truck manufacturers and farm equipment manufacturers.

Responsible for internal product development and coordination with technical liaison personnel in Germany and Japan, utilizing their expertise on complex development programs. Products, often assembled from imported components, were produced in a manufacturing plant in southern Illinois.

SAMPLE RESUME #2, PAGE 2

PROFESSIONAL EXPERIENCE (continued)

PRIVATE VENTURES AND CONSULTING   9/) 12/

                                                                  4   to 8/

    MANAGER OF MARKETING   (12/   to 8/
    MANAGER OF ENGINEERING AND MARKETING   (2/.   to 11/
    MANAGER OF ENGINEERING   (6,   to 1/
    PROJECT ENGINEER   (4/   to 5/

Division sales of $36 million in mid-1980 represented an eleven-fold increase since 1962, primarily due to aggressive new product development programs.

Directed Marketing Department including a direct sales office in Detroit, a group of representatives responsible for sales to the "Off-Highway" industry; and three Regional Managers responsible for OEM's, reps and distributors in their territories. Sales were to automotive, farm and construction, material handling and related OEM industries; and through aftermarket channels, to general industry.

Organized and directed Engineering Department consisting of 36 employees responsible for design and development, and technical upkeep of a diverse line of products including pressure switches, elapsed time indicators, flashers, and shock mounted lighting. The Department was particularly adept at timely, creative and cost effective development of new products.

    PROJECT ENGINEER   12/   to 2/

    PROJECT ENGINEER   2/   to 11,

EDUCATION

- Washington University, St. Louis, Missouri
  B.S.E.E.
- U.C.L.A. - Engineering and Management Course
- AMA - Marketing Management
- New York University - Mergers and Acquisitions
- Numerous seminars and additional courses

RELATED INFORMATION

- Hold 15 patents; very knowledgeable in patent law.
- Expertise in costs, costing, pricing and P & L matters.

SAMPLE RESUME #3

Business Summary

Fifteen years of managerial experience in electronics manufacturing, including six years of profit and loss accountability. Successfully implemented strategic plans, cost-reduction programs, improved current asset management and introduced and developed new products. Implemented numerous manufacturing and quality control procedures for compliance with government regulatory agencies. Functional managerial experience has also included responsibility in the areas of engineering, manufacturing and quality assurance.

Achievements

- Reduced average inventory by 25% ($500 thousand) and increased inventory utilization by more than 30%

- Achieved sales and gross profit growth of 7% annualized over a four-year period and contained operating expenses resulting in a compounded annual growth in operating profit of 14% over the same four-year period

- Implemented a program involving a 30% cost-reduction primarily in administrative overhead in response to a decrease in the demand for farm equipment and machinery in the marketplace

- Instrumental in the sale   Division. Completed sale in a timely fashion at targeted price. Directly involved in "due diligence" and all presentations to prospective purchasers.

- Installed new purchasing and material handling control system. This resulted in reduced overhead costs through elimination of dedicated MIS and improved response time by replacing existing batch system with on-line capability

- Established a test design department which included the hiring of personnel and acquisition of automatic test equipment as part of a new plant start-up with subsequent sales in excess of $100 million

- Introduced a division's first product lines utilizing hybrid thick film and surface mount manufacturing techniques

SAMPLE RESUME #3, PAGE 2

Employment History

Manufacturer of electronic instrumentation and controls.   19

    VICE PRESIDENT

Automotive electronics manufacturing.   19

    BUSINESS UNIT MANAGER   19
    PLANT MANAGER
    DIR., ENGINEERING & MANUF.   19

    19

Diagnostic equipment manufacturing.

    MANAGER, PRODUCT ASSURANCE

Consumer electronics manufacturer (formerly Consumer   19
Products Division).

    PRODUCTION ENGINEER

Education

Northwestern University (Evanston, IL)   19
    Master in Management Degree (concentration in International
    Business and Finance).

Illinois Institute of Technology (Chicago, IL)   19
    Master of Science, Electrical Engineering

Illinois Institute of Technology (Chicago, IL)   19
    Bachelor of Science, Electrical Engineering

Personal

Born   Ht./Wt. 5'8"/150 lbs.   Married, children

SAMPLE RESUME #4

NAME
ADDRESS
CITY, STATE ZIP
HOMEPHONENUMBER
WORKPHONENUMBER

OBJECTIVE — Executive level management position where I can utilize my operations experience to improve an organization's productivity and profitability.

EDUCATION — Bachelor of Science, Business Administration, Drake University, 1964.

EXPERIENCE

1964-Present

MANUFACTURING COMPANY, LOCATION.
A privately-owned manufacturer of drapery fabric and draperies with sales of $75 million consisting of four manufacturing plants and two warehouses.

1980-Present

Vice President of Contract Sales, Manufacturing Company, Location.

Responsibilities include:

- Development and expansion of contract sales division including customer interface, negotiations, and closure;

- Supervision of management information systems on Burroughs B-930, including development of comprehensive customized software.

Accomplishments include:

- Development and completion of major hotel project involving Japanese, resulting in $130,000 profit;

- Design and implementation of computer system for _____ including production and warehousing;

- Planned and implemented two physical moves of the company in 1983 and 1988, involving all aspects of site selection, design of office, warehouse and manufacturing areas, planning the physical move, equipment relocation and facilities preparation and inspection.

YOUR NAME, PAGE 2

1975-1980   **Chief Operating Officer**

Responsibilities included:

- Day-to-day management of company;

- Supervision of 55 individuals, including direct supervision of department heads in Warehouse, Production, Office Management, Management Information Systems, Controllership;

- Implemented program to become LEVELOR distributor. Negotiated LEVELOR contract leading to $2 million in sales;

- Developed manufacturing capability to produce vertical blinds including the review and determination of manufacturing capability and the selection and purchase of equipment;

- Planned and designed a new Burroughs B-700 computer system.

1970-1980   **Salesman**

Responsibilities included:

- Development of a program to promote sales of draperies and drapery hardware;

- Development of a Contract Drapery Program for the Sears Roebuck 400 Contract Division computer system including the design of a complete computerized warehousing systems and sales reporting procedures.

1964-1970   Various positions, including all facets of manufacturing, accounting, operations, maintenance and management information systems.

ACTIVITIES   Vice-President, _____ Homeowners Association
Vice-President, Ways and Means, _____
Member, Board of Trustees, _____
Recording Secretary: Executive Board of Board of Trustees, _____

INTERESTS   Running, weight-lifting, bicycling, duplicate bridge

REFERENCES   Available upon request.

SAMPLE RESUME #5

PRESENT ADDRESS: **PERMANENT ADDRESS:**

CAREER OBJECTIVE	Position in financial analysis or operations management with manufacturing, financial, or energy development corporation resulting in administrative career.
EDUCATION **1977-1978**	**Master of Business Administration,** December, 1978. University of Denver, Graduate School of Business and Public Management, Denver, Colorado. Course emphasis in finance and management. Course work included **Monetary and Fiscal Policy, Organization and Managerial Behavior, and Money and Capital Markets.** G.P.A.: 3.78
1973-1977	**Bachelor of Arts in Economics,** May, 1977. Tulane University, College of Arts and Sciences, New Orleans, Louisiana. Courses relating economics to business; finance, marketing, psychology courses. **Dean's List: Five Semesters, G.P.A.: 3.30**
EFFECTIVE SKILLS	Served as board member of community action organization, and co-chairman of community project. Scheduled and coordinated organizational activities, mediated between university and public school system, established college prep club at high school.
Administration / Supervision	Functioned as orientation coordinator for orientation program presented to incoming students. Planned activities, moderated discussions. Contributed to dormitory staff as resident assistant. Supervised activities of students in living environment, established regulations, implemented programs. Served as a laborer in water department of municipality. Changed water meters, repaired main breaks, instructed new laborers. Worked as laborer for woodworking company. Lifted objects for high-rise apartment building construction. Performed duties of lifeguard and swimming instructor for children's beginning and intermediate classes.
Business Consultation	Conducted group research on advertising and public relations techniques of specialty store chain and presented findings. Performed management study of beverage company. Submitted detailed report and presented information. Served as a business consultant for printing company. Developed structural reorganization of personnel program, implemented customer survey, cash-flow analysis, operating plan forecast.
WORK EXPERIENCE	**Intern Consultant,** Sir Speedy Instant Printing Center, Englewood, Colorado, April - August, 1978. **Intern Consultant,** Columbine Beverage Company, Denver, Colorado, January-March, 1978. **Laborer,** Water Department, City of Highland Park, Highland Park, Illinois, Summers: 1974-1977. **Intern Consultant,** Godchaux's. New Orleans, Louisiana, Spring, 1976. **Laborer,** Olsen Woodwork Company, Chicago, Illinois, Summer, 1973. **Lifeguard/Swimming Instructor,** Highland Park High School, Highland Park, Illinois, Summer, 1972.
ACTIVITIES AND INTERESTS	Board member, Community Action Council of Tulane University Students. Co-chairman, Project Opportunity. Orientation Coordinator and Resident Assistant, Tulane University. Member of Executive Committee, Graduate Business Students Association. Volunteer, United Way. Sigma Iota Epsilon-National Honorary Management Fraternity. Beta Gamma Sigma-National Scholastic Honorary Society for students of business and management.
REFERENCES	Available upon request.

SAMPLE RESUME #6

OBJECTIVE

Human resource management position which will allow exposure to employee development, training programs, and personnel administration.

EDUCATION

BRADLEY UNIVERSITY, Peoria, Illinois.
Master of Arts in Educational Leadership and Human Development, December 1984.
Bachelor of Science in Operations Management and Information Systems, May 1983.

EXPERIENCE

TRAINING and DEVELOPMENT
Operation Senior Security, Peoria, Illinois.
Trained senior citizens in human relation skills, simple counseling techniques, and reporting procedures.

RECRUITMENT
Bradley University, Peoria, Illinois.
Organized and implemented recruitment programs for two campus organizations. Developed recruitment materials, selection procedures, and interviewed candidates.

GENERAL
Bradley University, Peoria, Illinois.
Employed as a Graduate Assistant in the Development Office. Coordinated special parent/alumni events, advised the Undergraduate Association and provided staff support at University sponsored programs.

Stauffer Chemical, Chicago Heights, Illinois.
Worked in the motor storage department. Duties included assigning computer codes for inventories, assisting electricians, and maintenance.

ACTIVITIES

All-School Treasurer: Actively involved in campus activities representing the student body at meetings with University administrators including the president, vice-presidents, and controller.

Student Activity Budget Review Committee: Served as Chairperson directing eight students and five faculty advisors, responsible for allocating $100,000 to campus organizations.

Undergraduate Association: Redeveloped the organizational structure of the group. Established objectives, planned activities, and supervised 30 members.

All-Organizational Committee: Developed and implemented series of workshops designed to improve communication and interaction among campus organizations.

Skeleton Resume for Initial Resume Preparation

        Name: _____
        Address: _____
        Home Phone: _____
        Work Phone: _____

OBJECTIVE (Optional): _____
_____

EXPERIENCE:

DATES   POSITION: _____ COMPANY: _____

_____   LOCATION: _____

           COMPANY/DIVISION DESCRIPTION: _____
           _____

           RESPONSIBILITIES (Be as specific as possible):

           • _____

           • _____

           • _____

           ACCOMPLISHMENTS (Quantify as much as possible):

           • _____

           • _____

           • _____

DATES   POSITION: _____ COMPANY: _____

_____   LOCATION: _____

YOUR NAME,
PAGE 2

COMPANY/DIVISION DESCRIPTION: _____

_____

RESPONSIBILITIES (Be as specific as possible):

- _____

- _____

- _____

ACCOMPLISHMENTS (Quantify as much as possible):

- _____

- _____

- _____

EDUCATION:
DATES   DEGREE _____ , SCHOOL _____ ,

_____   LOCATION _____ ,

           HONORS/AWARDS/ACTIVITIES _____

DATES   DEGREE _____ ,SCHOOL _____ ,

_____   LOCATION _____ ,

           HONORS/AWARDS/ACTIVITIES _____

DATES   DEGREE _____ , SCHOOL _____ ,

_____   LOCATION _____ ,

           HONORS/AWARDS/ACTIVITIES _____

PERSONAL (Optional)
INTERESTS (Optional)
REFERENCES AVAILABLE UPON REQUEST

Cover Letters

There are probably as many ways to write a cover letter as there are people in the world. Since each person has his/her own style, you should follow your own approach. However, here are some guidelines for cover letters:

OBJECTIVES

- A cover letter is written to personalize the resume and therefore should describe your interests as well as providing the reader with an incentive to read your resume. A cover letter should never duplicate the resume. If it does, the reader will not have any interest in reading the resume in detail.

- A cover letter should be relatively brief and to the point. In very few cases should a cover letter EVER be longer than one page.

- A cover letter should describe:
  - Your objective
  - What you have to offer that is special
  - The timing of your request and follow-up.

Please see the six example cover letters on Pages 138-143.

COVER LETTER #1

To Whom It May Concern:

I am currently employed by _____. Consumer Household Products Division. We manufacture, distribute and sell _____ and other miscellaneous household cleaning products.

As the Manager of Warehousing and Inventory, I manage the national warehousing program including 13 public warehouses and private Chicago warehouse and also I oversee all the finished good inventories. In addition, I have extensive experience with _____ My enclosed resume details 12 years of experience in the logistics field.

I am seeking a new position with increased responsibility and an opportunity for long-term growth. I believe my recent successes (cost control) with _____ and extensive experience (production planning, warehousing and transportation) with _____ has prepared me for a position with increased national logistical responsibilities.

Your ideas and inquiries are welcome. My office telephone number is _____ 2246.

Sincerely,

COVER LETTER #2

Mr.

Dear Mr.

Is one of your present clients seeking to create a World Class Organization? If so, perhaps I can expedite their success.

Recent large gains in quality, customer service and satisfaction at _____ convinces me that a World Class company will create significant strategic advantages over its competitors. Owners and investors will enjoy dramatic improvement in Return on Investment through using the common sense World Class strategy.

Putting the customer on top of an organization chart and the CEO at the bottom supporting the efforts of everyone is a difficult yet rewarding process requiring vision and conviction. At _____ I personally identified the opportunity for continuous improvement and have championed the education and change process. I fully understand the intricacies of turning many of the values of an organization upside down.

We have done extremely well in regaining market superiority and profitability...so well in fact, that I am now seeking an even greater challenge so that I may provide significant value to yet another organization as General Manager or Chief Operating Officer.

If after reviewing your customers' needs you feel there may be a possibility for mutual benefit, I would enjoy talking with you.

Finally, although an exciting challenge is my objective, you should know that in recent years my total compensation has been in the range of $120,000 to $200,000.

Thank you for your consideration.

Sincerely,

encl.

COVER LETTER #3

Mr.

Dear Mr.

With a total of 23 years in the electro-mechanical and electronic industries, I am a senior level executive with experience in large as well as small manufacturing companies.

Skills

* Take charge leadership
* Team building
* Managing change
* Strategic development

Accomplishments

* Three business turnarounds
* Culture transformations to world class standards
* Assimilation of a $12 million acquisition
* Development of multi-product manufacturing strategies
* Product line relocations to off-shore
* Plant closures and consolidation
* Staff upgrades and rightsizing
* Identification and installation of MRP II systems
* Establishment of continuous flow manufacturing cells
* Development of global next generation product strategy
* Management of off-shore businesses
* Significantly improved profit, quality and customer service

Management Style

* Pro-active/participative
* People/team oriented
* Leader/motivater

I am exploring executive general management or operations positions with a total compensation in the low six figure range including base salary and performance dependent bonus.

A copy of my resume is enclosed for your review. I would appreciate an opportunity to meet with you should you have an appropriate search assignment.

Sincerely,

Enclosure

COVER LETTER #4

Mr.

Dear Mr.

I am a successful college graduate who is looking for the opportunity to continue to apply my proven skills in financial management, and general management.

I am writing because you may be in need of a man with my background and experience. If so, the following may be of interest to you:

    . I have the ability to lead and to work effectively with others under pressure in a goal-oriented business environment.

    . I have the intelligence, the capacity to learn, and the energy and drive to accomplish what needs to be done in a management position.

I have enclosed my resume and would like to meet with you to discuss further details of my career.

Sincerely,

COVER LETTER # 5

Mr.

Dear Mr.

Enclosed is my resume outlining over 20 years experience in manufacturing and materials management with the world's leading producer of luxury automobiles. My accomplishments have included:

- Improved vehicle quality by 42% and reduced warranty claims by 39%.
- Saved over $3 million in direct labor.
- Increased assembly line up-time by 6%.
- Developed and implemented a "state of the art" material flow system in a new plant start-up, as part of a core team.
- Co-designed and inaugurated a vendor selection process to allow for material to be supplied in-build-sequence.

I seek a Plant Manager or Director of Material position in a medium or large company. While I have particular expertise in the automobile industry, the skills and knowledge I have acquired are applicable to many fields of business.

Although I'm far more interested in a fine company and an intriguing challenge, you should know that in recent years my total compensation has been in the $90,000 to $100,000 range.

I would welcome the opportunity to discuss my resume in more detail and can be reached at my office   -   or at home number listed above.

Sincerely,

Enclosure (resume)

COVER LETTER # 6

Mr.

Dear Mr.

Please review the enclosed resume with respect to any current client assignments that match my experience and qualifications.

I am an Information Systems professional with over 20 years of progressively responsible experience and have managed major projects, both new design and development and package installation. As Systems Manager for Trust and Savings Bank, I installed a comprehensive trust accounting system which encompassed foreign exchange and multi-currency. I also led the design and implementation of nine interfaces during a two year conversion to a new domestic accounting system. Additionally, I was in charge of the local area network and PC group and oversaw a conversion from IMS/DB2 to a local area network. I also was project manager on the installation of a LAN imaging system.

Prior to I successfully completed assignments for Corporation as Manager of Special Projects, with conversions to MSA Payroll, Personnel, General Ledger and Accounts Payable systems.

I am interested in joining an organization — large or small — where my diverse systems and management expertise could be utilized. My current compensation is $75,000. If you have an interest, I would be pleased to hear from you.

Sincerely,

Enclosure

A fair exterior is a silent recommendation.

-Publilius Syrus
42 B.C.

Chapter 9 Fine Tuning Your Image and Behavior

We now turn to the "face to face" component of the personal marketing dimension: image. There are two types of image: internal and external. INTERNAL IMAGE is both what you <u>think of</u> yourself and how you <u>feel about</u> yourself. In more familiar terms, internal image is your "Self Image."

EXTERNAL IMAGE, on the other hand, is the <u>impression</u> you make on others. It is the opinion others form of you based on two factors: your appearance and your behavior.

External Image

We'll deal with External Image first. The first component of your external image is APPEARANCE. Appearance includes how you dress and how well-groomed you are. Your appearance is one of the two factors which, when combined, make an <u>immediate</u> impression on others. There are many books on how to "dress successfully." Suffice it to say here that you need to dress <u>appropriately</u>, which usually means conservatively, in the business setting, including when you go on a job interview, and to be well-groomed. (For further information, see the section in Chapter 11 titled: *Physical Image: A First and Lasting Impression*).

In this chapter, however, we concentrate on the second of the "impression" factors, BEHAVIOR. It is your behavior, that is, what you say and how you say it, and what you do and how you handle yourself, that is responsible for the <u>lasting</u> impression you make on others. Your behavior is the <u>effect</u> you have on others, either positive or negative. It is your behavior that causes others to make decisions about you, for example, whether to hire you into the organization or whether to advance and promote you within the organization.

What is your current EXTERNAL IMAGE? Let's find out. In the exercise below, circle any of the Descriptors that you feel you <u>currently project to others</u>, that is, the impression you think others currently have of you.

My Current "External Image"

SET 1

- Decisive
- Self assured
- Risk taker
- Result oriented
- Direct
- Assertive
- Quick

SET 2

- Persuasive
- Confident
- People intuitive
- Gregarious
- Enthusiastic
- Generous
- Optimistic

SET 4

- Conscientious
- Precise
- Systematic
- Diplomatic
- Accurate
- Analytical
- Discreet

SET 3

- Persistent
- Patient
- Deliberate
- Cooperative
- Empathetic
- Sincere
- Even-tempered

Now that you have completed this exercise, you may remember this list appeared earlier as the list of Work Style "Strengths" which you completed in Chapter 6. Set 1 describes strengths of the "Director" style, Set 2 the "Influencer", Set 3 the "Steady", and Set 4 the "Compliant". Your goal should be to review every one of the strengths listed on this chart that YOU DID NOT CIRCLE and make a decision now which of those strengths you will begin to learn how to portray. You want to be able to convince others that you have a variety of strengths which complement each other.

The following exercise will help you develop your "enhanced" external image. Write out below the specific strengths that you wish to learn to portray:

ENHANCING MY "EXTERNAL IMAGE": STRENGTHS I WANT TO ADD TO MY "SKILL SET"

_____

_____

_____

_____

_____

_____

Internal Image

The second type of image is Internal. It is your SELF IMAGE, (what you think and how you feel about yourself). Why is Internal Image important? It is your internal image which is the real cause of the impression you make on others. It is your internal image that PROMPTS all your behavior and your interaction with others.

For example, if you feel "down" on yourself, that "internal" feeling becomes "external" in the way you present yourself to others, including what you say about yourself and how you say it. Feeling "down on oneself" can be an issue for those who have lost their job, particularly if it takes a period of time to find a new one. Once you begin to blame yourself for losing your job you usually then begin to focus on your weaknesses and flaws rather than on your strengths and skills. Very soon this internal image you have of yourself starts to become external. You appear tentative, hesitant, unsure of yourself, and come to the interview with a sense of panic that this may be the last opportunity to find a job. Sometimes you may find yourself almost pleading to be hired. The external image you present to the employment interviewer will be quite negative and chances are you will not get the job precisely because of your negative internal image.

Contrast the above example with someone who feels self confident, optimistic and in control, a person who has identified and documented strengths and weaknesses, has prepared and rehearsed answers to potential job interview questions. The impression this person will make is much more positive and, while impression isn't everything, it certainly goes a long way to keep that person in the picture. This is especially important in terms of being invited to a second round of interviews.

What's the difference between these two individuals? The difference lies in their SELF IMAGE, negative in the first case and positive in the second.

The bibliography at the end of this Workbook provides you with references to a number of books which can assist you in improving your self image Look over this list <u>now</u> and choose at least one book to read (or reread if you've read it some time ago). Consider also obtaining and reading <u>Psycho-Cybernetics</u>, which, in our opinion, is the most significantly useful book available on improving your self image.

As a final exercise in this chapter, turn to the next page. This exercise will assist you in making a "game plan" <u>right now</u> which describes the image you think you are currently projecting to others and then identifies the image you<u> want to project</u> and specifies HOW YOU WILL GO ABOUT DOING SO.

Improving My "Internal Image"

Take some time to think about yourself and jot down your answers to the following:

1. What kind of image do you suppose you <u>currently</u> project in the work setting?

2. What kind of image do you <u>want</u> to project in the work setting?

3. Briefly describe your current self image.

   (Look at your earlier responses to the <u>WORK STYLE STRENGTHS</u> and <u>WORK STYLE WEAKNESSES</u> pages to assist you in answering this question.)

4. Write down at least five specific ways in which you can improve your own self image. "I want to..."

   4.1

   4.2

   4.3

   4.4

   4.5

Adding New Behaviors

Now that you have completed the "Image" section of this chapter, it is quite likely that you have identified one or more new behaviors you want to develop in order to improve both your internal and external images. If so, you have probably asked yourself, "Now what do I do?" While it is not within the scope of this Workbook to address in <u>detailed fashion</u> the topic of how to undertake change, we will provide you with a few observations and a simple yet reliable method for adding new behaviors.

First of all, be assured that change is QUITE POSSIBLE.

Change begins with your own AWARENESS of either your current external image or your current self image and, ideally, some awareness of the <u>effects</u> of your behavior. Our emphasis is on BEHAVIORAL CHANGE. Why? Because behavior, the primary component of your external image, is <u>easier to change</u> than attitudes or feelings, the primary components of your internal image. Behavior is the most <u>conscious</u> component of your personality. If you change your behavior then you AUTOMATICALLY, even though imperceptibly at first, begin to change your feelings and attitudes!

In order to begin the process of change you will want to identify specifically which behaviors you want to add to your "skill set". Refer back to your responses to the exercise, "My Expectations", in the Introduction of this Workbook, Page 8. This will help you in identifying new behaviors you might want to add.

It is very important that you start this process with ONE AND ONLY ONE new behavior. Do not try to change too much at once. Be patient. Otherwise, your efforts will be too scattered and therefore ineffective and ultimately frustrating.

Let's get started. Which ONE NEW BEHAVIOR do you wish to develop, starting now? Write it down below:

_____

This new behavior will become the content of "Step 1" of the exercise on the next page, "Adding New Behaviors."

Now, WHY do you want to add this behavior? What benefits can you expect from the change? Write as many benefits as you can think of that will be yours once you have developed the new behavior.

_____

_____

_____

_____

_____

_____

The benefits you have just listed will be utilized as you work through "Step 3" of the following exercise.

Adding New Behaviors: A Four-Step Change Process

There are two requirements for change to take place:

1. The DESIRE for change, and
2. A PROCESS to undertake change.

You have identified the personal attribute that you WANT to develop and thus have achieved the first requirement for change. Now, HOW do you achieve change? The following is an easy-to-understand process:

Step 1 Verbalize what you want to be or to have, not what you want to eliminate. In other words, state what you want in positive terms. For example, suppose that you want to change your feeling of being unsure of yourself in public. Rather than say, "I will no longer be unsure of myself," say, "I am self confident." Repeat this positive phrase to yourself many times each day.

Step 2 Visualize yourself as you want to be. Picture yourself behaving in a self confident manner. Provide as many visual details as you can.

Step 3 Energize your picture of yourself as you want to be. Use the "benefits" listed on the previous page to get yourself excited about making the change. Elaborate on your picture, including as many details as you can about how it feels, how it tastes, how it sounds, how it appears, how you conduct yourself and how you are positively received by others!!!!

Step 4 Actualize your vision of what you want to be. Act as if you are truly self confident, feel self confident, smile when you meet others, look forward to interacting with them. Begin NOW!!

Repeat this process several times a day over the next three weeks, the time it typically takes to establish and get comfortable with a new behavioral change. Then start on your next desired behavior which is:

_____

Nothing prevents our being natural so much as the desire to appear so.

-Francois, Duc de la Rochefoucauld

Chapter 10
Reading and Responding to Another's Work Style

You are now ready to consider the topic of how to "READ" other people in order to determine their work style. Then, once you have made your initial assessment of the other person's style, you need to consider how to ADAPT your behavior to communicate more effectively with that person.

In the last chapter we emphasized that you need to be aware of your external image, the effect of your behavior on others. Now we ask you to turn your attention away from yourself to other people and focus on becoming more PERCEPTIVE about the image that other people project to you! How do others project their image? It is projected by what they say and how they say it, in other words, by THEIR BEHAVIOR.

We will focus very specifically on relating and responding to the employment interviewer. The following page highlights a number of behaviors on a style-by-style basis which can help you identify the "style" of the interviewer. You might want to compare the behaviors of the others in your life against this chart. To do this, refer back to the "People in My Life" exercise in Chapter 3, Page 55, in which you listed the predominant style of various people.

Reading the Other Person: Key Behaviors of Each Work Style

DIRECTORS

- Impatient/restless
- Talks quickly
- Loud: wants to <u>dominate</u>
- Gets right to the point
- Interrupts others
- Makes bold statements
- Asks very few questions
- Quick to react
- Irritated by "rambling"
- Forceful

INFLUENCERS

- Demonstrative/animated
- Smiles readily
- Loud: wants to be <u>noticed</u>
- Uses small talk
- Very talkative
- Talks about self
- Asks "who" questions
- Optimistic
- Enthusiastic
- Manipulative

COMPLIANT

- Contolled/unemotional
- Emphasizes facts & data
- Revels in details
- Speaks slowly & precisely
- Listens, but skeptically
- Asks "why" questions
- Exacting
- Aloof/cool/detached
- Critical
- Communicative only when <u>sure</u>

STEADY

- Pan faced
- Slow paced/easy going
- Nondemonstrative
- Speaks softly & sincerely
- Listens well
- Waits until acknowledged
- Asks "how" questions
- Patient, takes time
- Friendly but low-keyed
- Methodical

While it is important to learn to "read" others, it is also wise to go into the employment interview with a "WORKING HYPOTHESIS" about the work style of the interviewer you will be facing. This will give you an INITIAL SET OF EXPECTATIONS AND BEHAVIORS to have at hand as you begin the interview.

Having dealt with hundreds of interviewers, we present the following as a "working hypothesis" about the work style of employment interviewers you will face.

If you are about to be interviewed by an **executive recruiter** you can expect the work style in descending order to consist of:

- Director
- Compliant
- Influencer
- Steady

On the other hand, if you are about to be interviewed by a **human resource specialist** you can anticipate the work style in descending order to be:

- Compliant
- Steady
- Director
- Influencer

Notice what these two different recruiters HAVE IN COMMON: the "Compliant" style — facts, no stretching the truth — and the "Director" style — get to the point, be logical, look and act "in control".

It is our suggestion that as you go into the interview you be fully prepared to deal with both the "Compliant" and the "Director" styles, which, in fact, are the most difficult styles for many people to deal with. Then, if during the course of the interview, you realize that the "Steady" or "Influencer" styles are being utilized by the interviewer, adjust your behavior accordingly.

It will probably be easier for you to deal with the "Steady" and the "Influencer" styles than to deal with the "Compliant" or the "Director" styles because the former are more relaxed and friendly and try to put the interviewee at ease, while the latter prefer to get right down to business.

To ensure a successful interview, therefore, be sure to DO YOUR HOMEWORK — BE PREPARED — AND PRACTICE!!

Let's look now at "responding to" each of the four styles. The chart on the following two pages provides some KEY BEHAVIORS tailored to make you more effective with each of the four styles. Study this chart closely. Compare the chart with the exercise you completed in Chapter 3, Page 55, on the predominant styles of others in your life. Ask yourself, "Would the responses listed on the following page be effective with each of those people"? Then start to practice each of these behaviors PRIOR TO the time you go to your next job interview.

Proactively Responding to Each Work Style

With DIRECTORS

- Always speak to the point
- Speak rather quickly
- Show you're in control
- Give overview answers
- Don't go into detail unless asked
- Emphasize how you "take charge"
- Emphasize that you get things done
- Focus on what you've <u>accomplished</u>
- Show enthusiasm for your work
- Say how you focus on "bottomline"
- Emphasize that you solve problems

With INFLUENCERS

- Be openly friendly; smile
- Say you're sensitive to people
- Ask questions to prompt them
- Say you <u>enjoy</u> your work
- Emphasize "open" communication
- Mention who you may know
- Stress the customer comes first
- Say how well <u>they're</u> doing
- Stress your work <u>motivation</u>
- Engage in small talk
- Say you believe in high morale

Proactively Responding to Each Work Style, (cont'd)

With the COMPLIANT

- Emphasize your work <u>quality</u>
- Say you take <u>pride</u> in your work
- Tell how well you're <u>organized</u>
- Provide all relevant details
- Focus on <u>tasks</u>, not on people
- Address all their questions directly
- Be accurate and precise
- No small talk or emotionality
- Say that you can work on your own
- Don't try to "bluff" your way

With the STEADY

- Say you work step-by-step
- Be agreeable; smile
- Say you can figure out "how"
- Describe your <u>loyalty</u>
- Show interest in them
- Emphasize your <u>cooperativeness</u>
- Say you're a "team person"
- Speak rather slowly; don't rush
- Say how you "fit in" to the group
- Say you like to master a job

Do your homework so that you are fully prepared to discuss every aspect and to respond to every question and comment.

-Benjamin Franklin

Chapter 11 Preparing for Your Interview

Interviewing, from the point of view of the one being interviewed (the interviewee) is 75% science, 25% art. By this we equate the "science" to the research, self analysis and advance preparation that must be invested by the successful interviewee. The 25% "art" comes into play in terms of the style of delivery by the interviewee during the interview. This may include nuances in terms of word use, articulation, carriage, and body language, among other things. The truly successful interviewee knows how to meld science and art into a COMPLETE, POLISHED PACKAGE.

First, please describe below your view of what comprises a successful interview (in terms of you, the interviewee):

_____

_____

_____

_____

_____

_____

_____

_____

What did you write down? Organized thoughts? Clear answers/statements? A positive attitude? All these issues, and many more, are important to the successful interview. Let's look at the different types of interviews on Pages 173-176. No matter which type of interview you are pursuing, there are components which are universal which will result in greater interview success. Let's discuss these in detail.

Physical Image: A First and Lasting Impression

Most of us realize that physical carriage, including the way we look, our personal grooming, the style of our clothes, and other physical attributes comprise our physical image. This image is absorbed by others in a face-to-face meeting within a very short time. In the personal interview, this image is evaluated by the interviewer within the first five minutes of meeting the interviewee. Opinions are formed quickly and a "physical concept" of the person is established in terms of an initial impression. Publilius Syrus, (circa 42 B.C.) stated it very well when he said: "A fair exterior is a silent recommendation."

In terms of the interview setting, simplicity is the name of the game. This means that appropriate attire should be worn for the particular position that you seek.

If you are interviewing for a professional position such as a business position, it is customary for women to wear a business suit or dress, while men should wear a suit and tie. The key here is to dress in keeping with the position and the attire of the interviewer. For instance, if the interviewer will be wearing a sport shirt and sweater, it may make more sense to dress in the same casual manner so as to not feel out of place.

When it comes to other aspects of physical carriage, be certain that your clothes fit properly, that colors match, that your choice and application of cologne or perfume is not overwhelming, and that you and your clothes are clean. If your interview requires that you leave town, always pack an extra shirt or blouse in case something spills on you or you are trapped for hours in a poorly ventilated airplane or car on the way to the appointment. In this way your outfit will appear clean and pressed no matter what the situation. In addition, be certain that your shoes are well-polished. Many people make the mistake of not concerning themselves about their shoes' appearance, but a worn or dull shoe takes away from an otherwise sharp appearance. In today's competitive employment marketplace YOU CAN'T AFFORD TO APPEAR LESS THAN YOUR BEST DURING THE INTERVIEW PROCESS.

The Value of Advance Preparation

Most interviewees make one terrible mistake: they let the interviewer know, in effect, how little they care about the specific job opportunity by being poorly prepared. This lack of preparation comes in many forms. In many instances it is demonstrated by the poor quality of questions asked by the interviewee at the end of the interview.

This is particularly true of college students, who have a penchant for asking questions which can be better answered by reading corporate brochures or other literature. For instance, questions such as "Please tell me more about your corporate benefits plan" exhibit a lack of preparation as well as a lack of insight by the interviewee. Strange as it may seem, many interviews are ruined by the interviewee's asking simple or obvious questions.

This is true at even the highest levels of the corporate world. We have interviewed many candidates for MANY DIFFERENT positions over the last twenty years. A surprising percentage don't have a true understanding of the company or the position for which they're applying. Because they are unprepared, they exhibit a nonchalance towards the position which ultimately hurts their chances of being pursued further.

DON'T LET THIS HAPPEN TO YOU! When asked why you want to work for a specific company, you must try to be as discerning and knowledgeable as you can.

Don't ever answer "Because I like to work with people." This is a "stock" answer for college students and is perhaps the worst answer that you could give. It is viewed as an admission to the interviewer that you haven't done your homework in preparing for the interview and that you are merely "out interviewing" versus choosing a specific niche. Even experienced businesspeople make the mistake of not establishing several specific reasons for the company to hire them. In other words, THEY DON'T SELL THEMSELVES. If you don't sell yourself in the interview setting, WHEN ARE YOU GOING TO DO IT?

Regardless of your level of experience, the interviewee should make certain that he/she has RESEARCHED the specifics of the company. This is very easy if the company is publicly held, as information about the company is usually readily available through the company's Office of Shareholder Services or the Treasurer or Chief

Financial Officer. Information available includes the Annual Report, the 10-K and 10-Q statements and related documents. In addition, this information is readily available in the library through Moody's or Dun & Bradstreet's reference manuals.

While this information regarding the company's financial performance, structure and strategic objectives may be tougher to access for privately held firms, there are resources that can assist you.

Your best bet is to visit your local library and ask for assistance in finding the appropriate reference source by contacting the Reference Librarian or the Librarian in charge of the Business Section. Or, you can call the company to see if any literature about the company, such as a brochure or product information, can be sent to you.

Know Yourself

When preparing for the interview, be certain that you have a solid handle on the components of your self that we discussed in earlier chapters in this book. This preparation and self-knowledge will provide you with an excellent foundation for performing successfully in the personal interview.

In addition, ask yourself the following questions:

- What is the interviewer most likely to ask me?

- Can I answer all the expected questions succinctly and with a sense of purpose as well as with solidly organized thoughts?

- Are there any chronological "holes" in my background which are likely to be discovered, and if so, can I clearly discuss and defend these without appearing to cover them up?

- When I present my qualifications, do they sound credible, well-organized and solid? Am I enthusiastic or just matter-of-fact?

- Have I predicted and planned my responses to the questions that I am likely to be asked? (Please see the list of potential questions on Pages 176-178).

- If I were interviewing "myself", what impression would I provide as an interviewee?

These questions, and your ability to answer them with a degree of self-confidence should provide you with excellent insight into your level of preparation for your next interview. One effective technique for improving your interviewing skills is the Practice Interview. Before you begin the practice interview, review the "Suggestions for a Successful Interview" on Pages 179 and 180.

You will recall that in Chapter 9 on Page 150, you completed an exercise on your "internal (self) image". Take time now to think about your IDEAL INTERVIEWEE IMAGE. That is, think of the specific physical attributes, carriage, quality of answers and approach that you would like to portray in the interview setting.

Example: I would like to be viewed as an excellent candidate. This entails being relaxed, yet interested. My facial expression should be serious, but convey openness and honesty. I will try to exhibit enthusiasm, etc. etc.

Now, write your own IDEAL INTERVIEWEE IMAGE below:

_____
_____
_____

_____

_____

_____

_____

The Practice Interview

The Practice Interview can be conducted alone or with another person. It is generally more effective with someone else.

If it is done alone, it should be conducted in a private place, and can be effectively performed in front of a mirror in order to view your physical presentation. There you can modify facial expressions, critique your eye contact and expand or contract your answers to "practice" questions.

If performed with a partner, you must first ask a friend that you trust to take the role of the interviewer. Provide that person with a list of questions that should be asked as part of your Practice Interview. Practice responding to these questions so that your answers are credible, straightforward, reasonably detailed, but brief. Ask your partner to comment on your performance in terms of eye contact, voice control, body language, attentiveness, and organization skills.

Keep practicing, with or without your partner, until you feel comfortable with the quality of your responses. Ask your partner to critique your style. Let your partner read what you wrote as your IDEAL INTERVIEWEE IMAGE and comment on whether or not you appeared to fit your "Ideal

Image" during this practice session. Then modify your approach to fit this image more closely. The secret to interview success is the Four Ps:

- PREPARATION
- PRACTICE
- PATIENCE
- PERFORMANCE

Understand Your Audience

In terms of interviewing success, you have prepared yourself very well by completing the exercises and readings in this workbook. In addition, it is important to try and "pick up" cues from your interviewer. If you are interviewing in the individual's office, your task is much easier. Try to be as observant as possible when you enter the office. Is the office modern or traditional? Are there any diplomas, plaques or other notable objects on the wall? How about books?

All of these articles provide insight into the tastes, interests and experience of the interviewer. If you absorb this information, COUPLED WITH WHAT YOU NOW KNOW ABOUT INDIVIDUAL WORK STYLES, chances are that you will find it to be very valuable in terms of your interview. If you are especially fortunate, you may even find a diploma or certificate from a school or course that you attended. Use this information to establish a bond between you and the interviewer. "A sense of place" is typically a great area to discuss, especially if you went to the same school, were raised in the same area, etc.

Finally, try to BE YOURSELF. No matter how much advance preparation you undertake, you still should represent yourself as you are. After all, if you secure the position, you will feel much better about "the fit" if you have come across as you really act on a day-to-day basis. Don't forget the value of the Work Style Profile to assist you in your view of yourself and of others.

The Most Common Types of Interviews

Informational Interview

In this interview, the interviewee attempts to get together with the interviewer for the purpose of learning more about the company and the potential opportunities which may exist. The interviewer normally is making an accommodation, either because the interviewee has convinced him/her, or (more likely) because the interviewer has been asked by a mutual contact to do a favor and see the interviewee.

In this setting, it is important to be very cordial, and to err on the side of being brief. Interviewers and other human resources professionals are generally very busy. Try to generate interest in your background and convince the interviewer that your credentials are worth a closer look, either by him/her, or better yet, by a line professional.

Screening Interview

The screening interview is a very common method to rank qualified interviewees for a particular position. Normally it is conducted by one person, is short in duration and results in either a rejection letter or a more in-depth interview at a later date.

Frequently, the screening interview is conducted by telephone as a means of separating qualified candidates from those that do not fit the bill for a particular position. It is often the second phase of the screening process after the initial review of the resume.

As a candidate, it is important to answer succinctly, with crisp, well-organized responses, as time is usually limited in either the telephone or face-to-face version.

One-on-One Interview

The one-on-one interview is very common and involves the interviewee and only one company representative (or search professional). The interview normally lasts from one hour to ninety minutes and very often follows a format which is decided upon in advance. This format is often the result of the specific concept of the position that is being filled.

A key issue to consider in this interview is the length of your answers, as the interviewer usually has a large amount of information to gather. If you must pursue open-ended questions such as "Tell me about yourself", try to move the interview along by shortening your answers and forcing the interviewer to ask follow-up questions. This will help to prevent the interview from dragging.

Group Interview

The group interview is utilized relatively often in higher level positions where the candidate needs to be approved by the Board of Directors of a company or by an entire committee.

The group interview often involves the candidate fielding questions from several different individuals in sequence, with the interviewee expected to move swiftly from one question to another. The group interview is often used as a term to describe an interview variant: the Multiple Sequential Interview, which we discuss next.

The key to success in the Group Interview is remaining calm, and providing substantial industry as well as technical knowledge. This is often a prerequisite for positions of significant authority such as CEO or President. The crux of this interview is to try and satisfy all parties, as the decision on a specific candidate is often by consensus of the entire committee.

Multiple Sequential Interview

The Multiple Sequential Interview is a series of consecutive interviews conducted by different individuals that comprise an interview team. These interviews are usually conducted within a period of the same half day or full day. Each interviewer can have his or her own agenda, or more often, has an agenda of questions which fits the overall agenda of the group. In this way, the risk of duplication in content from one interviewer to another is minimized.

The members of the group normally complete evaluations and then compare their notes at the end of the day to determine how the candidate fared in his/her sessions.

Stress Interview

Although less common than it was ten years ago, the stress interview is still used by certain organizations either on an individual basis or as part of the Group Interview. The rationale for the stress interview is simple: create enough stress for the candidate during the interview to cause reactions similar to what might occur under pressure conditions on the job. This is achieved either by having many people fire questions at the interviewee or by one person firing questions. Normally, responses are chopped off or ridiculed by the interviewer. The interviewee's responses are then observed and critiqued as to their content and emotional control.

This technique normally serves to alienate the interviewee, and results in the opposite effect than is intended: it causes the interviewee to "clam up" instead of open up. Consequently, its use is of questionable value. As a public relations tool, it can only serve to hurt the organization that utilizes it.

Sample Interview Questions

- Tell me a little bit about yourself.

- Is there a person in your life that you consider most influential in terms of your success?

- Describe your three most significant accomplishments.

- Describe your strengths and weaknesses.

- Describe your ideal work environment.

- Have you ever had a person as a supervisor that you would consider a mentor? If so, please describe that person. If not, can you describe the characteristics of your ideal superior?

- How would your superiors collectively describe you?

- How would your subordinates collectively describe you?

- How would your peers collectively describe you?

- Describe what frustrates you most in terms of your current (last) position.

- Where do you see yourself headed in the next three to five years?

- What distinguishes an outstanding (accountant or example position) from one that is merely mediocre?

- Do you have any regrets regarding your choice of career?

- If you had the chance to do it all over, would you have chosen the same career? If so, why? If not, what would you choose?

- What principles of life most influence you day to day?

- Tell me about your interpretation of business ethics.

- Please describe your management style.

- How does your management style compare to that of your superior?

- Please describe the culture of your current (most recent) organization.

- Please discuss a major project that you had responsibility for.

- What do you look for when you hire someone?

- Please describe the individuals in your department.

- Can you provide an example of anyone that you have hired that has developed beyond their "initial hiring position"?

- Why do you want to work for this company?

- What can you do better than anyone else?

- Describe your best friend.

- How have you taken steps to improve upon what has been stated to you in your performance appraisals?

- Why are you interested in leaving your current position?

- Describe a famous individual that you consider to be most significant to you in terms of influencing your life.

- Tell me about your outside activities.

Suggestions for a Successful Interview

- Visualize your success in advance. See yourself in the interview performing capably and in a relaxed manner.

- Prepare yourself by practicing responses to key questions.

- Present an image of poise and control, while maintaining a high level of self-confidence.

- Establish yourself as technically competent in your field by answering questions and asking questions with sufficient depth and understanding so that there is no doubt in the mind of the interviewer.

- Present a physical image which is clean, crisp, professional and well-coordinated.

- Watch your choice of phrases and words carefully; don't use words that you are unsure of just to try and impress the interviewer. Many candidates, even those that are highly educated, misuse words in interviews.

- Measure your responses so that you don't appear too verbose or too succinct. Realize that the interviewer will usually ask a follow-up question if he/she wants you to expand on one of your answers.

- Many interviewers don't ask interviewees directly to "sell themselves". Be certain that you have a planned amount of information that you will "deliver" in terms of selling yourself. Be creative as to when you will "slip in" the information.

- Establish a pattern of practice; use either a partner or a mirror (or both). Be certain to practice eye contact, as it is an area that most people need to improve.

- Prepare thoughtful questions in advance by researching the specifics of the company, including financial performance, history, product categories, and growth.

- Prepare post-interview notes as to your feelings regarding the interview. Be critical of your responses and think of ways that you can improve for the next interview.

- Write the interviewer a follow-up letter which demonstrates your continued interest and thanks him/her.

Summary: Your Journey Continues

Let's face it: Preparing for the rest of your life is a rigorous task. But your diligent application of the exercises in this workbook, along with continuous updating of your thoughts and ideas, will provide you with the mental development, self-knowledge and self-confidence to face each day with renewed optimism. And hopefully, it will lead to a position which is ultimately rewarding, challenging, and genuinely enjoyable. If you succeed in this endeavor, just think how satisfied you will feel!

You've started the journey of discovery that carves a path which is the right one for you and you alone. While there will always be obstacles along the way, you should find comfort in your abilities. Not only do you have strengths, which are unique, but you have the capacity to learn continuously. And through learning more about yourself and what is best for you, you'll be able to achieve CAREER SUCCESS.

Thank you for purchasing the workbook. We hope that you have enjoyed it. It is the product of our lives' work. We owe a great deal to the students in our courses, our individual clients, other authors in a variety of fields, our friends and our families for their insight and honesty regarding today's job market and its effect. We wish you well on your new road of discovery. May yours be a journey of excitement!

JOHN ELSON & DICK WRIGHT
AUGUST, 1992

TO CONTACT ELSON/WRIGHT ASSOCIATES:

We welcome your comments and suggestions regarding our workbook. We would like to hear from you regarding areas that you enjoyed or that you feel may need clarification. Please contact us at:

ELSON/WRIGHT ASSOCIATES
ROLLING MEADOWS OFFICE
3306 SOUTH ORIOLE LANE
ROLLING MEADOWS, ILLINOIS   60008
708-398-0640

Research List
A Partial List of Potential Sources of Information

American Hospital Association Guide To The Health Care Field

American Institute of Certified Public Accountants

America's Corporate Families — The Billion Dollar Directory

Best's Insurance Reports

Crain's Top Business Lists

Crain's Who's Who In Chicago Business

Directory of Corporate Affiliations

The Directory of Directories

Directory of Directors

The Directory of Executive Recruiters

Directory of Multihospital Systems

Directory of Top Computer Executives

Encyclopedia of Associations

Everybody's Business — An Almanac

First Chicago Guide

Health Care Financial Management Association Directory

Hospital Management Systems Society Yearbook

Illinois Manufacturers Directory

Illinois Services Directory

Research List, cont'd

Moody's

Nelson's Directory of Wall Street Research

Other States' Manufacturers Directories

Rand McNally Bankers Directory

Standard & Poors Register

Who's Who in the Midwest

A Suggested Reading List

Anthony, Dr. Robert. *Total Self Confidence.* New York: Berkley Books, 1979.

Branden, Dr. Nathaniel. *The Psychology of Self Esteem.* New York: Bantam Books, 1987.

Berne, Eric, M.D. *Games People Play.* New York: Ballantine Books, 1964.

Castaneda, Carlos. *Journey To Ixtlan.* New York: Simon & Schuster, 1972.

Cohen, Herb. *You Can Negotiate Anything.* New York: Bantam Books, 1980.

Covey, Stephen R. *The Seven Habits Of Highly Effective People.* New York: Simon & Schuster, 1989.

Dyer, Wayne. *Pulling Your Own Strings.* New York: Avon, 1977.

Fritz, Robert. *The Path of Least Resistance: Learning How To Become The Creative Force In Your Life.* New York: Fawcett Columbine, 1989.

Helmstetter, Dr. Shad. *The Self Talk Solution.* Studio City, California: Dove/Morrow Books On Tape, 1988, (Audio Cassette).

Johnson, Raymond C. *The Achievers.* New York: E.P. Dutton, Division of New American Library, 1987.

Maltz, Dr. Maxwell. *Psycho-Cybernetics.* New York: Pocket Books, 1969. (Also available on audio cassette).

McGregor, Douglas. *The Human Side of Enterprise.* New York: McGraw-Hill, 1960.

Suggested Reading, cont'd

Morrisey, George. *Getting Your Act Together: Goal Setting For Fun, Health and Profit.* New York: John Wiley & Sons, Inc., 1980.

Peck, M. Scott, M.D. *The Road Less Travelled.* New York: Simon & Schuster, 1978.

Prather, Hugh. *Notes To Myself.* Moab, Utah: Real People Press, 1970.

Robbins, Anthony. *Unlimited Power.* New York: Fawcett Columbine, 1986.

Rusk, Tom, M.D. and Read, Randy, M.D. *I Want To Change But I Don't Know How.* Los Angeles: Price Stern Sloan, 1986.

Von Oech, Roger. *A Whack On The Side Of The Head: How You Can Be More Creative.* New York: Warner Books, 1990.

Index

Appearance, 145
Behavior:
    Adding new, 151-153
    Definition, 146
    Others' behavior, 157
Career Assessment, 38
Change:
    Process of, 152-154
    Requirements for, 153
"Compliant" Style, 54, 158
Cover Letters:
    Purpose of, 137
    Samples, 138-143
"Director" Style, 51, 158
Dislikes:
    Integrating with Strengths and Weaknesses, 98-102
Documentation, 22
Favorable Environment, 108
Group Interview, 74
Image:
    External, 145-147
    Internal, 145, 148-150
    Physical, 166-167
"Influencer" Style, 52, 158
Informational Interview, 173
Intangible Tangibles, 41
Interviewers, employment, 157, 159
Interviews:
    Practice interview, 171
    Preparing for, 167-169
    Questions to ask, 169-170
    Suggestions for, 179-180
    Types of, 173-176
    Typical questions asked, 176-178
Introspection, 22
Job Search Log, 113-114
Job Profiling:
    Current job, 66
    Ideal job, 69

Likes:
   Integrating with Strengths and Weaknesses, 98-102
Maltz, Maxwell, 149
Marsden, William, 108
Master Career Planning:
   Aspects of, 21
   Components of, 12
   Example, 28
Mission Statement, 29
Multiple Sequential Interview, 175
Networking, 114
One-on-one Interview, 174
Planning, 26
Proactivity, 26, 105
Progress Review, 26
Reading others, 157-160
Reflection, 23
Responding to others, 161-162
Resumes:
   Chronological, 117
   Format, 135-136
   Length of, 119
   Overview of, 117
   Purpose of, 119-120
   Samples and Critiques, 121-134
Screening Interview, 173
Self Check, 34
Self Image, 148-149
Skills:
   Charting, 86-87
   Definition, 73
   "Functional", 74
   Key Skill Areas, 75
   Multilevel definition of, 81, 84
   "Personal", 74
   "Technical", 73
"Station, The", 18
"Steady" Style, 53, 158
Strengths:
   By Work Style, 78
   Definition, 77
   (See Skills).
Stress Interview, 176

Tangible Tangibles, 39
Unfavorable Environment, 108
Weaknesses:
   By Work Style, 79
   Charting, 88-90
   Multilevel definition of, 81, 85
Work Style:
   Interaction among, 57
   Overview, 50
   Strengths of, 78
   Weaknesses of, 79

About the Authors...

John Elson

John B. Elson, M.B.A. has served in the management consulting field for more than 13 years.

Prior to establishing his own company, THE ELSON GROUP, INC., he was a Senior Manager in the Executive Search Practice of a major multinational consulting firm. Before that, he served as Assistant Director of Recruiting for an international, Big Six, public accounting firm. His early experience includes significant consulting work in information systems, including systems review, planning, design and programming.

He has conducted seminars, workshops and presentations in many different arenas, and has consulted with organizations in both the for-profit and not-for-profit sectors. He has assisted organizations in the manufacturing, distribution, financial services, insurance, health care, and government areas. His experience includes assisting more than one hundred individuals to improve their career paths through assessment and training. He has been a featured speaker for the Wisconsin League of Savings Institutions, the Northern Illinois Chapter of the National Multiple Sclerosis Society, Northeastern Illinois University, and the Greater O'Hare Association Free Enterprise Council.

He began teaching in 1974 as a volunteer instructor in the New Orleans Public School System. He is currently an Adjunct Continuing Education Faculty member of the College of Lake County and Wilbur Wright College. He is a frequent contributor to local publications on a variety of subjects related to recruitment and career strategy.

His academic credentials include a Master of Business Administration degree and a Bachelor of Arts degree in Economics.

Dick Wright

Dick Wright, Ph.D. has served in the organizational development field for over 20 years.

Prior to establishing his own company, WRIGHT DIRECTIONS, INC., he was Corporate Director of Strategic Planning at Alexian Brothers Health System, Inc. and was Director of Management and Organizational Development at Loyola University of Chicago. He has also served as a high school teacher, guidance counselor, and administrator.

He has conducted hundreds of seminars and workshops throughout the country before top executives, board members, middle managers, supervisors, support staff, and has undertaken a variety of consulting assignments in both the for-profit and not-for-profit sectors. He has been the featured speaker at national meetings of the American Society of Training and Development, the Learning Resource Network, the Image Industry Council International, the American Society of Clinical Pathologists, the American Medical Record Association, and the American College of Healthcare Executives.

Adjunct Professor of Business at Elmhurst College and of Human Resource Development at Northeastern Illinois University, he has served on the continuing education faculty of Loyola University of Chicago, and conducts ongoing education programs at William Rainey Harper College, the Chicago City Colleges, and McHenry CountyCollege.

His academic credentials include a Doctorate in Educational Administration and Masters degrees in Counseling and in Business Administration.

If you want more...

▶ Additional copy of the critically acclaimed **CAREER SUCCESS WORKBOOK**. 191 pages of concepts, ideas, and exercises ranging from MASTER CAREER PLANNING to INTERIEWING SKILLS. $14.95 per copy. **Product Code: BK-0001**

▶ An essential companion to the CAREER SUCCESS WORKBOOK, the **Computerized Version of the Workstyle Profile** will generate a three-page report describing your style, tendencies and "environmental preferences". It comes complete with a descriptive page to help you interpret *your* three graphs. Chapters 3, 4, and 10 of the CAREER SUCCESS WORKBOOK discuss the concepts related to this product in great detail. When we receive your order, we will send you the self-evaluation form to complete *(it takes only ten minutes!)* and return to us. When we receive your completed form, we will send you your THREE-PAGE INDIVIDUALIZED REPORT within one week. $7.95 per copy. **Product Code: WS-0001**

▶ Additional copy of the **CAREER SUCCESS WORKBOOK** (BK-0001) *including* the companion **Computerized Profile** (WS-0001). $19.95 complete. *Save $2.95 by buying both!* **Product Code: BK-0002**

✂ --

▶ ☐ I'm not buying any of these products today, but please add me to the Elson/Wright Associates **MAILING LIST** so that I will receive information on other products/services. I have completed the name/address portion below.

Tell us what you want...

Product Description	Product Code	Quantity	Cost per Item	Line Total

Tell us how you'll pay...

SUBTOTAL

☐ Check/Money Order Enclosed
☐ VISA ☐ MASTERCARD

Illinois residents, add 6.5% sales tax _____

Shipping/Handling

_____
CARD NUMBER

_____
EXP. DATE

Total Order	S/H
Under $10	➜ Add $2
$10.01 to $20	➜ Add $4
Over $20	➜ Add $6

Name _____

TOTAL

Address _____

City _____ **State** ___ **Zip** _____ **Phone (___)** _____

If this is a gift, please provide the proper mailing information.

Ordering is easy...

📞 Phone 708-317-0200 **OR** ✉ Mail this form to Elson/Wright Associates, 3306 S. Oriole Lane, Rolling Meadows, IL 60008.
We ship all orders within one week! (This form may be photocopied).